D0910264

GLASS
CHILDREN
AND
OTHER ESSAYS

GLASS
CHILDREN
AND
OTHER ESSAYS

DAISAKU IKEDA

translated by Burton Watson

KODANSHA INTERNATIONAL LTD.
Tokyo, New York & San Francisco

Distributed in the United States by Kodansha International/USA, Ltd. through Harper & Row, Publishers, Inc., 10 East 53rd Street, New York, New York 10022. In South America by Harper & Row, International Department. In Canada by Fitzhenry & Whiteside Limited, 150 Lesmill Road, Don Mills, Ontario M3B 2T6. In Mexico & Central America by Harla S.A. de C.V., Apartado 30–546, Mexico 4, D.F. In the United Kingdom by Phaidon Press Limited, Littlegate House, St. Ebbe's Street, Oxford OX1 1SQ. In Europe by Boxerbooks Inc., Limmatstrasse 111, 8031 Zurich. In Australia & New Zealand by Book Wise (Australia) Pty. Ltd., 104–8 Sussex Street, Sydney 2000. In the Far East by Toppan Company (S) Pte. Ltd., No. 32 Liu Fang Road, Jurong, Singapore 22.

Published by Kodansha International Ltd., 2–12–21 Otowa, Bunkyo-ku, Tokyo 112 and Kodansha International/USA, Ltd., 10 East 53rd Street, New York, New York 10022 and 44 Montgomery Street, San Francisco, California 94104.

LCC 78–65720
ISBN 0–87011–375–5
JBC 0095–787103–2361

First edition, 1979

CONTENTS

PREFACE

Time goes by so fast. Most of the essays in this volume were written seven or eight years, or even a decade, ago and originally published in Japanese newspapers and periodicals. They take as their theme some event or topic prominent in the news at the time. Reading them over now, however, they seem to deal with a period far more remote than a mere decade ago.

But if the events dealt with belong now to past history, the ideas that I tried to express remain the ones I hold today, and I do not think I will have occasion to change them to any great extent in the future. The present English translation therefore gives me the chance to place some of my ideas and ways of looking at things before the readers of the world, an opportunity that I regard as both a privilege and an honor.

As I explained in the Japanese edition of one of the collections from which these essays are taken, I am neither a historian nor a critic of world civilization. If pressed for a description, I would call myself a man of religion, a Buddhist, and a member of the common people. The views and the outlook expressed in these essays are certainly not representative of the present-day Japanese population as a whole. What they do represent are the ideas of one rather average Japanese, a man born and raised among the common people, who does his best to live his life day by day. And because I am by no means unique, they also represent the thinking of at least one among the several types of Japanese today.

We are often told that, although Japan is widely recognized throughout the world these days for its economic power, Japanese culture, and in particular Japanese ways of thinking, unfortunately remain almost wholly unknown abroad. The blame, it is said, lies in the peculiar ineptness of the Japanese in explaining their ideas and aims to others, or their poor training in foreign languages. I think it also stems from the fact that in the past the Japanese have had rather few opportunities to present foreign readers with a frank and open exposition of their views.

The publication of these essays of mine in English offers such an opportunity, and if it serves in some degree to acquaint the people of other countries with the Japanese mind and heart, with the mental and emotional dimensions of the people of Japan, then it can perhaps perform a valuable service.

At the present time we are confronting various crises of unprecedented scale and complexity. The greatest need at this moment is for all the peoples of the world to pool their wisdom and strength in working to surmount these difficulties. The basic prerequisite for such a cooperative effort, I believe, is mutual understanding.

Differences in the history and background of nations and peoples, as well as the varied nature of the particular cultures they have evolved, often act as barriers to mutual understanding. And yet, paradoxically, it is precisely this varied nature of human culture that holds out the possibility for overcoming the crises of the present and opening up a way for the future, for, as mutual understanding increases, each culture and nation will be able to make its own unique contribution, creating in time a new wisdom and power of a magnitude never dreamed of before.

In the past I have done my best to transcend the barriers of East and West, socialism and capitalism, which divide the people of the world today, and to establish bonds of mutual understanding. And I intend to devote the remainder of my life to this endeavor, doing whatever is in my power, little though it may be. It is my hope that the present volume will serve in some degree to further that end. If it does, I will feel myself richly rewarded for my efforts.

In closing, I would like to thank Professor Burton Watson for the time and effort he spent in preparing the English translation of these essays.

TRANSLATOR'S NOTE

English translations of some of these essays appeared earlier in a volume entitled *Yesterday, Today and Tomorrow*, Robert Epp, tr., World Tribune Press, 1973. In making my own translations of the same essays, I have profited greatly from Dr. Epp's versions, and I would like to take this opportunity to acknowledge my debt and my gratitude.

THE UNIVERSE
AND HUMAN LIFE

In recent years, ever since man began launching satellites into space, his ideas about the universe have been undergoing a profound though little noticed change.

The science of astronomy has existed since ancient times, yet when we as children in Japan looked at the full moon, we invariably saw in it the image of a rabbit pounding glutinous rice to make rice cakes—because that was what adults had told us existed in the moon. The adults, we learned later, had told us a lie. But even the adults, when they looked at the full moon, particularly in the autumn, probably had thoughts almost as stereotyped as ours, thoughts like those expressed as early as the Heian period by the ninth century poet Ōe no Chisato in his famous verse on the full moon:

When I gaze at the moon
all things seem sad,
though I know the autumn
comes not to me alone.

For modern man the moon has, in terms of intellectual understanding, become quite familiar and near at hand, though in terms of its suggestiveness, the emotional power reflected in Chisato's poem, it has become strangely remote. Fantasies about a rabbit pounding rice will soon disappear entirely, and in the space age of the not too distant future, children looking up at the full moon will probably say, "My daddy's staying up there tonight. I wonder what he'll bring me back for a present?"

In this coming age, the ones who will probably suffer most will be the

11

poets, for whether they like it or not, the emotions associated with the moon are bound to undergo a drastic change. For all we know, the famous poems of the past which had the moon as their inspiration may come to seem like so many dreams or illusions. As far as the poets are concerned at least, it is a sad age we are entering, one in which the fictions associated with the moon are about to give way to hard fact.

This change has come about in a period of only a few years. We all remember the stir of excitement and amazement caused by the launching of the first satellite, the Soviet Union's Sputnik 1, ten years ago (on October 4, 1957). For a while the whole world talked of nothing else, and people commented to each other on the astounding progress of science with such frequency that it began to sound like a form of greeting.

At that time, when all the rest of us were in such a commotion, I remember a wise man's reprimanding us for it. "There's no cause to get so excited," he used to say. And he would add with a laugh, "One more tiny little star up in the sky, that's all!"

He did not live to see the launching of Apollo 8. If he had, he would undoubtedly have looked upon that event with the same calm detachment. Recently I have come to understand the source of his unruffled attitude; it derived from the view of the universe he held in his late years, a view based upon the truths of Buddhism.

Buddhism explains the process by which the universe is formed in terms of the four *kō*, four kalpas or vast eras of time. It is a theory based upon a keenly intuitive understanding of the nature of the universe and one which I am convinced will in time be verified by the findings of science.

This theory envisions the universe as going through an endlessly repeated cycle of four kalpas or eras, the *jōkō* or Kalpa of Formation, the *jūkō* or Kalpa of Continuance, the *ekō* or Kalpa of Destruction, and the *kūkō* or Kalpa of Emptiness. The universe is thus seen as a single entity, all of its parts being subject to the same four stages of transformation. The period during which this world is taking shape is the Kalpa of Formation. When this process is completed, the universe enters the Kalpa of Continuance, which is marked by a continuation or sustaining of the conditions prevalent at the time of its origin and the appearance of plant and animal life. We today are living in the Kalpa of Continuance. This in time gives way

12

to the Kalpa of Destruction, when the form of the universe is gradually destroyed, and is followed by the Kalpa of Emptiness, during which nothing exists at all. Each kalpa lasts for an indescribably long period of time, and once the entire process has been completed it begins again, the Kalpa of Emptiness being followed by a new Kalpa of Formation.

This remarkable view of the universe seems to have been propounded as early as three thousand years ago, and would appear to be related to the concept of transmigration. In this view, the life of the individual, his physical being, represents no more than one single event or entity existing within this eternal process of transformation. Once a man has grasped this fact, he cannot but turn his thoughts to the eternal recurrence of the life force within him as it manifests itself over the periods of past, present, and future. Thus it comes about that in Buddhism, a view of human life has evolved which sees it as basically an inseparable part of the universe as a whole.

The life of a single individual may therefore be seen in the same terms as the life of the universe. From the time when the embryo is first formed in the womb, through the period of birth and adolescent growth, may be likened to the Kalpa of Formation. The period of vigorous adult activity that occurs upon the completion of growth corresponds to the Kalpa of Continuance. Old age follows, comparable to the Kalpa of Destruction and ending in the death of the individual. After death, the life force melts into the universe, entering the state of the Kalpa of Emptiness, in time to undergo transmigration and enter once again upon the Kalpa of Formation. Thus it seems clear to me that, although the life of the individual and that of the universe differ astronomically in terms of the number of years required to complete one cycle, the basic principles governing the four-stage life of the universe and the four-stage life of the individual human being are precisely the same.

This Buddhist view in time led to an overall philosophy of life, which had as its basic premise the identity of the individual and the universe. But this fundamental principle has remained, over the several thousand years since its inception, as no more than an intuitive insight lacking scientific proof of its validity.

Since the beginning of the twentieth century, however, the findings of science have step by step moved toward a picture of the universe that

13

comes remarkably close to the traditional one expounded in Buddhism. The first thirty years or more of the century were ones of dramatic discovery and change, particularly in the field of physics. First, Einstein's theory of relativity completely revolutionized the concepts of time and space derived from the old system of the Newtonian laws of motion and gravity, and in doing so necessarily altered our conception of the universe as well. Later came the quantum theory, which cast new light on numerous areas, from the structure of the atom and its nucleus to the motions and process of formation of heavenly bodies.

These rapid developments in the area of theoretical physics in the present century have had a staggering effect on the field of astronomy. The theory of the evolution of the fixed stars has been put forward, a theory which in effect offers proof to support the concept of the four kalpas. And now we have the Gamov theory of the evolution of the universe, which proposes to explain how primal matter exploded, expanded, and through the force of gravity was shaped into the form of nebulae. It no longer seems possible to view the universe as the creation of a deity or deities. Such theological explanations have now quite lost their luster. In their place another intuitive view of the origin and nature of the universe, one founded upon the concept of the life force, has risen like a phoenix from the ashes of the past to command the attention of men of the twentieth century. Modern science, though certainly without any conscious attempt to do so, seems to be moving closer and closer to the traditional Buddhist philosophy of life. Thus the twenty-first century, as its civilization progresses and unfolds, may come to be noted not only as an era of great scientific advancement, but as the century of the life force.

Beginning my remarks with the tale of the rabbit pounding rice in the moon, I have contrived by some means or other to arrive at this rather unexpected and far removed point. What I really wish to emphasize is the fact that these changes in the way in which we view the universe are, in my opinion, also bound to exercise an enormous influence upon our view of human life. If we are in fact about to enter upon a new age in which travel through space is accepted as an everyday matter, then it would seem only natural to suppose that the cruel wars and conflicts that continue to rage on earth will before long come to appear as stupid and petty as a boundary dispute with the house next door. And perhaps we will also come to our senses and realize that, since the Kalpa of Destruction in any event lies in wait for us in the future, hastening things along by attempting to blow the world apart with nuclear weapons is worse than senseless.

The view of the universe held by modern science has advanced, one might say, to the very threshold of the four-kalpa theory, but it has yet to attain a view of the universe which, like the four-kalpa theory, sees it as a process of repetition, beginningless, endless, and eternal.

A sage of former times remarked that the revolutions of the universe are infinitely compassionate. This view of the universe, which is at the same time a view of human life, will eventually come to be understood and accepted. I am convinced of it.

THE ARROGANCE
OF THE PRESENT

"Alienation," "dehumanization," "loss of humanity" . . . It has been some time since people began to bandy such terms about. No one seems to tire of them. They go on being repeated and repeated until now they have sunk to the level of intellectual jargon, expressions blunted in meaning and grimy with use.

How often one hears people, observing the obtuse, disspirited crowds of men and women of our time, say in a solemn and knowing tone, "A typical case of dehumanization!" They never seem to notice the lack of feeling in their own voices as they say it. Not only are they unaware of their own coldness and lack of humanity but, like some tribe that has never learned the use of mirrors, they go so far as to look with scorn on others who are in trouble or distress. It is in this spectacle, repeated daily, that the true unhappiness of modern society is revealed, often with a clarity verging on the comic. And isn't it true that modern man's inordinate pride and arrogance only make the situation worse?

I have been around for forty years, and I have never yet found the leisure to worry about whether I was becoming alienated or whether others have become dehumanized. At no time and under no circumstances have I ever doubted the reality of myself and others as human beings. But by concentrating my attention upon the various forms which that reality assumes, I have come to understand how, by changing the destiny of one individual in the world today, it becomes possible to change the destiny of all mankind. Armed with that knowledge, and with the aid of prayer, I have tried to do my best in one way and another to combat and overcome the miseries that beset the globe today.

16

From the point of view of the universe as a whole, it seems a small matter, one that concerns only one tiny corner of that universe. Human wisdom has advanced to the point where man can construct satellites; only a few days ago one circled the moon and came back to earth safely. I call that a real achievement. And yet man in his wisdom cannot find a way to rescue an old woman in Vietnam from her tragic plight. We can't wait to find out what the pockmarked face of the far side of the moon looks like, but we have no time to consider what meaning those wrinkles of sorrow etched deep into the face of an old woman may have for us. We have come to think of war, the greatest of human catastrophes, as some sort of natural disaster. Then we try to ease our consciences by busying ourselves with refugee relief. In the end it is not war that is the disaster. Far more disastrous is this puffed up little creature of modern times called man.

Before long men will no doubt succeed in landing on the moon. The problem of student unrest in the universities, the incident in Czechoslovakia, the stalled Vietnam peace negotiations—in areas where human wisdom is most needed, it seems to be least in evidence, and so the suffering and discontent are prolonged or even intensified. What is the reason for this channeling of human wisdom into certain areas alone? Doesn't it seem peculiar that we can solve the mysteries of the universe and the heavenly bodies and yet are unable to solve the mystery of a single human being?

When it comes to the question of their own identity as human beings, the men and women of today seem to me to be wholly irresponsible. Though they can see with their own eyes the miseries abundant in modern society, they somehow believe such problems can all be solved by that little bag of tricks known as government. For this pride and overconfidence they will have to pay a heavy price some day.

To be sure, the researches carried out in the natural sciences in modern times have spurred the development of disciplines directly related to the study of man, such as physiology, psychology, biochemistry, and sociology. And no one can deny that, as a result, human life has in many ways been improved and made more pleasant. But at the same time we have discovered that the higher the level of material advancement in their immediate environment, the more prone men are to suffer from

17

spiritual malaise and discontent, a wholly unexpected phenomenon before which science stands mute and bewildered.

Unless serious and concerted efforts are made to study and understand this strange being we call man, and the life force that propels him onward, then the men and women of modern society can, unfortunate as it seems, move in only one direction, that which leads to their extinction. Man in the mysterious strangeness of his being has in the past devised a number of different religions. In their appraisal of human problems and the solutions they offered, however, these religions out of an excess of exclusiveness have departed too far from the beaten track and in most cases lost themselves in mazes of doctrine, becoming the deceivers rather than the saviors of mankind.

If there is a single ultimate principle of truth underlying the workings of the life force, then it is reasonable to suppose that there is in similar fashion a single religion capable of explaining the life force. I believe it is the urgent duty of the men and women of the present age to learn to assess the relative profundity and sophistication of the religions about them and make this their first step toward a study of the strangeness and mystery of this being called man.

Modern man must set aside his arrogance and in a spirit of true humility apply himself to the study of the life force and the human being.

AUTUMN IN PRAGUE

I arrived in Prague, in the midst of my first trip to eastern Europe, on the first day of autumn, 1964. On that day, the Olympic Games commenced in Tokyo.

I boarded a plane in Paris for Prague. Since it belonged to the Czechoslovak Air Lines, in effect I was already in a corner of eastern Europe. The scheduled departure time arrived, but for some reason the plane did not move. About forty minutes later, three men who looked as though they were high officials in the Czech government entered the compartment, scowled at the other passengers, and took their seats with an air of unconcern. Only then did the plane taxi out onto the runway. Apparently the high officials of the Novotny government had sufficient authority to delay the takeoff of an international flight for the better part of an hour.

Prague struck me as gloomy. Perhaps it was just the solemn atmosphere cloaking the buildings of the old capital. And yet, particularly coming directly from Paris, I couldn't escape the feeling that there really was something dark and melancholy about the expressions of the people walking along the streets. As though they were constrained, even cowed by some unseen power, many of them wore the masklike expressions of men and women who have forgotten how to laugh. It struck me unexpectedly, and I wondered if this was the true face of the socialist states established in the postwar period.

After settling myself in my room at the Yalta Hotel, I went to the hotel coffee shop. There a crowd of people was gathered around a television set, watching the opening ceremonies of the Tokyo Olympics as they were relayed by satellite. Since less than half of the crowd looked as though they might be guests at the hotel, I concluded that the remainder must be ordinary citizens of Prague. The fact that they had assembled here suggested that very few families owned their own TV sets. Though Czechoslovakia is the leading industrial state of eastern Europe, the life of the ordinary citizens, one would judge, is far from affluent.

My purpose in coming to Prague was to purchase materials for use in the construction and decoration of the Shō-Hondō of the Taisekiji at the foot of Mount Fuji. I therefore decided to take a walk around the city to see what I could find in the stores. I was particularly interested in the glassware for which the country has so long been famous, and was hoping to find a beautiful chandelier to decorate the ceiling of the Shō-Hondō. But, perhaps because the summer tourists had already bought up everything of worth, I could find nothing in any of the stores that interested me. Not being able to carry out my original objective was a considerable disappointment.

The next day, I set out from the hotel for a brief walk before breakfast. As I strolled along the streets of the city in the chilly morning air, I noticed a poster advertising the Tokyo Olympics plastered on the stone wall of a house. The sight of the poster, which I had seen so often in Japan, was also unexpected. I stopped in front of it, seized with a sudden feeling of homesickness. Presently I became aware of a tall young man standing behind me. He seemed to be about twenty-five or twenty-six, with rather lonely eyes staring out from his youthful face. Remembering I had some of the hundred-yen coins minted to commemorate the Olympics in my pocket, I took one out and gave it to him. When he held the coin in his hand and saw the five-ring symbol of the Olympics in the light of the morning sun, he gave a little cry of surprise and broke into a cheery smile.

The young man began fumbling through his pockets, at the same time asking rather apprehensively how much I wanted for the coin. "I'm giving it to you as a present!" I said. He looked at me with an expression of disbelief. When my little gesture of friendliness finally got through to him, his face changed completely. He grinned with the innocence of a child. I wondered if he was starved for something as simple as an open and friendly greeting. If so, how lonely the citizens of Prague must be. All at once it came to me that perhaps the lives of the people of Czechoslovakia are controlled by some powerful force, carefully hidden from view but never to be forgotten or trifled with.

With a busy schedule ahead of us, I and the others in my party had to leave Prague after only one night and go on to Hungary. But the vivid memory of that autumn day in Prague remains with me today.

Some days ago we were suddenly confronted with the news of massive Soviet military intervention in Czechoslovakia. When I heard of it, the first thing that flashed through my mind was the appealing face of that young man. A few days later the newspapers carried pictures of youths leaping up on Soviet tanks and waving Czech flags. I wondered what had happened to that young man, his innocent grin hidden behind an outward air of sadness. Perhaps now, his face flushed with anger, he had seated himself in protest in the path of the tanks. In any event, I found that the sorrows of the Czech people for some reason moved me with particular force.

After returning from that trip in 1964, I could no longer feel indifferent to the course of events in the eastern European countries I had visited. And when, in the autumn of the year before last, a Japanese translation of *Delayed Report* by the Czech writer Ladislav Mnacko came out, I took the opportunity to read it.

A collection of superb short stories based on actual incidents, the book was published in 1965 and in no time had sold some 300,000 copies—this in a country whose total population is only thirteen million. Reading the book and considering its remarkable sales, I was more impressed than ever at how strongly determined the Czech people are to fight for freedom of speech. At the same time I wondered what influence the book would have upon the country and just how that influence would be manifested, and determined to keep a watch on the situation. As it turned out, of course, the Novotny regime fell from power and a heretofore unknown leader named Alexander Dubcek came to the fore. From the beginning of this year, the country suddenly began moving with accelerating speed in the direction of greater freedom. The leaders in the movement were all members of the Writers' Union, and the banner they marched under was that of freedom of speech.

The characteristic of this Czech movement toward liberalization, as I see it, was the insistence that all reforms in the areas of economics, poli-

21

tics, etc. must first of all be carried out on the basis of a freedom of speech in which facts are openly proclaimed and recognized as such. The Russians, realizing that in a socialist state the power of free speech is more to be feared than the threat of an atomic bomb, apparently felt that they had no choice but to intervene with military force, regardless of what moral censure they might incur or how world opinion would react.

When men, though aware of the facts, are not only deprived of the freedom to discuss them openly, but must spend their whole lives mouthing untruths, it is only natural that their spiritual nature as human beings should undergo drastic and frightening changes. How long can men endure the suppression of free speech? That, perhaps, is something that can best be divined from the follies of the numberless powerful men of history who have attempted to suppress it. And it is the accumulation of their follies, one should note, that in the end has brought about their destruction.

In most capitalist countries at the present time the citizens are free to discuss facts as facts. At the same time, however, men with sufficient power seem to enjoy the further liberty of utilizing freedom of speech to spread lies in the guise of truth. Citizens in socialist countries of course have no such freedom to discuss facts. What is more, the power holders are at liberty to tell lies in a perfectly open manner, and this is what is looked upon as "freedom of speech." Anyone who stops to think about it will realize that there is something radically wrong with the situation. And it is a distortion which is causing unhappiness to hundreds of millions of people on the earth today. When men come to realize this, perhaps they will understand just how necessary freedom of speech is as a condition for human happiness, and will be prepared to defend it with their lives.

Delayed Report, one might say, simply presents the facts as they exist. It pictures men in the process of realizing their ideal of building a socialist state, and shows just how many honest ones among them are made fools of and how many liars manage to rest secure in the seat of power. The wise people of Czechoslovakia, knowing how great the importance of freedom of speech is, had just begun, in the period before the Russian intervention, to set about working toward the solution of the various problems in their society, moved by a new spirit of elation. The clash between the Czech people and the Soviet troops represents in a sense the conflagration ready to break out at the point of contact between the two great areas of truth and falsehood that blanket the world today.

At the moment the fire seems to be merely smoldering. But I have no doubt that the sagacious Czech people, in order to pursue their fight for what is right, are expending both sweat and tears. Autumn must be at its height in Prague now.

POVERTY AND WEALTH

Once more the season has come around for the Liberal Democratic Party to elect a new president. Onlookers who take an interest in such things will no doubt have a number of critical comments to make. To anyone who is familiar with the true state of Japanese politics and is sincerely concerned about the corruption characteristic of the political arena, the carryings-on of the Liberal Democratic Party can seem only farcical.

What is wrong with Japan today? Anyone can tell you. It has to do with the fact that, while in terms of the productivity of its people it ranks third in the world, in terms of annual per capita income it ranks no higher than a disappointing twenty-third. In the harsh fact of this discrepancy is summed up the whole situation of present-day Japan.

Should Japan be called a wealthy country or a poor one? Looked at as a whole, the islands of Japan would seem to be the most prosperous nation in all of Asia. Yet anyone who takes the time to question the Japanese as individuals will find that this illusion of prosperity quickly vanishes.

In its place one finds a mass of ordinary people, most of whom are obliged to live jammed together with their families in houses that are far too cramped and who have to make do with meals low in calorie content. Perhaps there are just too many people and that is what is dragging down the average income? Perhaps if measures were taken to reduce the population through mass emigration the individual income would climb? That of course is absurd, even supposing it were possible. After all, is it not precisely because this excessively large population is willing to work like ants that the country is somehow able to maintain

24

its position as third in the world in terms of overall productivity? If there were fewer people, then surely the level of productivity would fall, would it not? There is no end to such mathematical imaginings.

The poverty of the common people, a great problem in prewar Japan, has continued to be a problem in the postwar era as well, and, sad to say, it seems to resist all efforts at solution. During the Meiji period, in the latter part of the preceding century and the first part of the present one, the government labored to modernize the country, summing up its aims in the slogan, "Enrich the nation and strengthen the military." But all the ardor of the government leaders seems to have been devoted to carrying out the latter part of the slogan, until there emerged the militaristic and ultranationalistic regime of the years immediately preceding the Pacific War, whose sole objective seemed to be to "impoverish the nation and strengthen the military." Though founded upon an anomaly to begin with, the regime attempted one impossible feat after another until, in an act of complete madness, it set the country upon a course of total destruction, one which it pursued with fearful speed to the expected conclusion.

Japan in the postwar period, awakened from its nightmare of militarism and freed from the burdensome expense thus imposed, should, according to all normal calculations, have been able to establish itself as an advanced nation in which both the individual citizens and the nation as a whole could enjoy a comfortable degree of affluence. No one would deny that the nation has in fact prospered. And yet the majority of the citizens continue as before to live in a condition of poverty, struggling under the burden of excessive taxes. Today, twenty-three years after the end of the war, Japan has achieved a condition rare among the countries of the world, that of a rich country with a poor citizenry.

It is easy enough to blame all this upon a poverty in the quality of government itself. But if one is to accuse government of impoverishment or lack, one must consider just where it may lie. It seems to me that there is no lack of government policies, nor is there a shortage of persons to implement them. The problem lies in the poverty of the political ideals of today's politicians. From impoverished ideals one can never expect anything but impoverished government.

Among the politicians in power there are undoubtedly those who spend restless nights worrying about the possibility of being investigated on charges of corruption, and others who ponder how to maneuver success-fully through the days ahead. But is there a single one who is willing to face the seemingly insoluble problem of a rich country with an impover-ished citizenry and spend a few sleepless nights agonizing over that? I doubt it. While these men, in the midst of the rapidly shifting conditions of the world, have their little moments of triumph and despair, they have totally abandoned anything worthy of being called political ideals.

With the naiveté of children they talk of nothing but taking shelter under the "nuclear umbrella" of another country. The earth revolves and man-made satellites can go anywhere. It will not be long, I feel sure, before they can successfully journey to the moon and back. Where, then, in what corner of this narrow globe, is one to find anything so convenient as an umbrella, nuclear or otherwise, under which to hide?

Essentially, it is the target of their thinking which has become unfocused. Correct concepts or ideals can come into being only when one's thinking is correct. Is the point to be simply the advancement of oneself as an individual, or is it to be the cause of world peace? Is it to be the mainte-nance of the power of one particular class in society, or, even worse, the venting of hatred and the invasion of another country? The focus of the thinking will determine everything that follows. Men are capable of conceiving ideas that are grand and lofty, and those that are petty and mean. Therefore, there is no need to despair just because the realities of the situation seem forbidding. Man is never entirely without hope; in this respect he is a very fortunate animal. Where there is thinking that is correctly oriented, there will be correct ideals, and correct ideals will surely lead to correct government.

A rich country with a poor citizenry: anyone who is willing to face this inescapable reality of present-day Japan and examine it with unpreju-diced eyes—anyone who makes it the point of his thinking—is bound to conclude that the prosperity of society as a whole and the happiness of the individual must be regarded as inseparable. A hopelessly visionary ideal, you may say. But I believe that if we persist in demanding its realization, then some lofty and farsighted conception will come into being in re-sponse to that demand, and that conception will be carried out in practice.

If the country grows rich, it is only reasonable to suppose that the individual citizens will grow rich as well. How, then, are we to account for this imbalance in the case of Japan? Is it because Japan is a country so poor in natural resources that it must import most of what it needs from abroad? There are many other countries in the world which are poor in natural resources and still enjoy a high standard of living. But to be third in terms of productivity and only twenty-third in terms of per capita income—surely this discrepancy is too great. The crisis facing our country is not one of national security, as so many people seem to believe. The source of the danger, in my view, lies precisely in this ominous and persistent discrepancy.

For some reason, the interests of the poor people of Japan are being sacrificed. Politicians who fail to perceive this, who simply go on appealing to the people for thrift and social harmony, deserve to be labeled nothing more than scarecrows. Clever sparrows, once they learn that they are dealing with scarecrows, soon cease to be awed. It is only to be expected, then, that the people of this country should in the same manner cast a contemptuous eye at their scarecrow politicians.

Is there any politician today who is truly concerned about this discrepancy and is sincerely trying to work out some practical plan to improve the lot of the general public? To worry constantly about whether the balance of trade is running in one's favor or not is hardly the way for a great financial power to behave, yet that is what the Japanese government is doing today. The ordinary citizens of the country are the real sufferers in this tragic situation, working away as industriously as ants, setting aside a little money in savings, and entrusting everything else to the government.

In any event, the fact is that we are faced with this discrepancy. And it tells us, whether we like it or not, that if we ever hope to escape from the present anomaly of a rich nation and an impoverished citizenry, we must begin to think of the prosperity of the society as a whole and the well-being of the individual as inseparable goals, and begin step by step to work out some practical means of attaining them. If man has the mental capacity to solve the problems of space travel, he certainly must be capable of coping with this much more urgent and immediate problem of how to harmonize the interests of the individual and of society. And yet no one in a position of political power today seems willing to give serious thought to the matter.

27

GROWTH RINGS

Another year is drawing to a close. Each year at this time we exclaim on how stormy and eventful the year has been, until it begins to sound like a cliché. Cliché or not, we can hardly help taking notice of the events of the year 1968.

First came the assassinations of Dr. Martin Luther King and Robert Kennedy. The whole world responded with shock and sorrow, as suddenly for a moment we glimpsed the darker side of American democracy. In France the train of events that began with student riots led in time to a national crisis, and just when we thought that had passed, all of Europe was shaken by a failure of confidence in France. It was certainly far from being a year of glory for France. I suspect I am not the only person these days who, watching the sun set in the late autumn sky, sees in it a reflection of the waning fortunes of Europe as a whole.

In Japan, as the riots and unrest in the universities drag on, countless promising young men and women expend all their energies learning how to practice violence. Meanwhile, classes are at a standstill, and though the present frightful year is about to end, no one as yet seems to have the slightest idea how to remedy the situation. It would appear that the peace and tranquility of former years will never return to the wrecked campuses of our country. We can only comment that the impoverishment of the human spirit is proceeding at a faster rate than anyone could have predicted.

I could go on to mention any number of other gloomy incidents, but to tell the truth, I haven't the heart for it. When men cease to think constructively and turn their energies to destruction, how fearful the results can be! Appalling as it is to contemplate, they may even consider resorting to nuclear warfare. There is nothing subtler and yet more powerful than men's determination. It is the determination of the individual which drives him to pursue the goal he has fixed upon, whether it be right or wrong.

In spite of all the turmoil, there were a few welcome events in the course of this year. Step by step, progress in the space program brought man closer to a landing on the moon. In addition, talks began in Paris in an attempt to reach a peaceful solution to the Vietnam War, and bombing attacks on North Vietnam were finally halted. Though a natural enough decision to make, America wisely began at last to apply the brakes on its involvement in Vietnam. Japan in its involvement in China before the Pacific War neglected to apply the brakes. As a result, the hostilities continued to widen and widen until in the end the nation was engulfed in a tragedy that all but destroyed it. If at the time of the China Incident some kind of truce had been arranged, Japan and the other countries drawn into the Pacific War might have been spared the subsequent horror and destruction. In this sense we might say that America is more fortunate than Japan was. In any case, events offer further proof of how unimaginably great is the power of human determination, whether for good or for evil.

If society were, in the manner of a tree, to grow annual rings, with the occurrences of that particular year clearly reflected in the shape and pattern of the ring, I wonder what sort of ring the year 1968 would leave behind? I doubt that it would be a pretty one. More likely it would be an unsightly affair, scarred with anguish and full of random and incoherent markings.

What a contrast to the annual rings one observes in a cross section of a tree, each one beautiful in its own way. Concentric circles rounding in forceful curves, one within another, they record the history of the growth and development of the tree, laid down one by one by the intrepid life force of the tree as it struggled to withstand the winds and snows of many passing years. These rings reflect the progress of cell division. Variations in the density of the cells cause a new ring to be added with each year of the tree's growth. The circles in effect are created by the changing seasons. In spring and summer, when the process of cell division is proceeding

29

most rapidly, no striations are formed in the wood. In autumn and winter, when cell division becomes much less active, a series of curved striations are formed, delicate and compressed but clearly defined. The annual rings tell the entire story of the tree's life, and the minute waves in the concentric circles reflect variations in its day-by-day existence.

It is interesting to note that trees growing in environments where there are no changes of season form almost no rings at all. As one proceeds from subtropical regions to the tropics, the annual rings formed by the trees become gradually fainter and less distinct, until they disappear entirely in trees growing in the tropics. In this sense, the annual rings are actually records of the bitter winters endured in the course of a lifetime.

When a tree encounters some sudden change in the environment, such as a spell of unseasonable weather, or when it is subjected to severe insect damage, it may create two rings in the course of a single year. These pseudo-annual rings are the subject of intense study by climatologists, for they allow the observer to calculate exactly when major changes took place in the natural world. The tree rings are above all honest, and their honesty constitutes a kind of style and beauty distinctively their own.

Man too is bound to have his annual rings. Bivalves year by year add new striations to their shells, and the scales of fish in like fashion show yearly lines of growth, both annual rings of a sort. Though no such lines are found in the human body, if one were to search for some counterpart, he might find it in the changes that take place in the lines and contours of a person's face. And end up wondering why the kind of grandeur and beauty that would bear comparison with the annual rings of a tree are seldom encountered in a human face.

Lincoln understood this about faces when he made his famous remark to the effect that anyone over forty must take responsibility for his own face. When one calls to mind that lean and bearded face of Lincoln himself, one knows what he had in mind. His face indubitably possessed the kind of beauty and distinction reminiscent of the growth rings of a great tree. It is the beauty of one who has stood up against, and weathered, the storms of many long years. It's not just my imagination; the years of growth are clearly marked in his face.

One can observe the same thing by comparing photographs of Tolstoy when he was a young man and when he was old. While the youthful

Tolstoy may have had the face of a genius, it was a rather undistinguished and commonplace countenance compared to that of his old age. As he grew older, however, his face took on an increasing air of nobility. It was a face he was prepared to take responsibility for, one clearly marked with the growth rings of a lifetime. It was in no sense a face in which could be seen comfortable maturity and self-satisfaction, but rather that of a man who lived life earnestly and intensely, a face that bespoke none of the ugliness of old age.

If there is any part of the body that reveals the years of a man's life, it must surely be the face. Perhaps the wrinkles and convolutions in the brain reveal them as well. I rather imagine the brain as taking on beautiful formations like those of growth rings. But we cannot look inside the brain, whereas the faces of ourselves and others we can always examine. The wrinkles in the face correspond, I suppose, to the striations of the growth rings. Yet the wrinkles in the human face most often suggest sorrow and the meanness of old age. It is rare indeed that one encounters a face with truly beautiful wrinkles in it.

My intention in this essay was to talk about the ring added to the globe by the year 1968, but somehow I have gotten off onto the subject of the growth rings of the individual. Readers with a sense of responsibility who are over forty might, as they prepare to greet the new year, find it interesting from time to time to glance into a mirror at the growth rings on their own faces. Have any of you tried it? What did you see?

But I shouldn't always be telling other people what to do. Since I was born in 1928, I will soon have passed forty myself.

THOUGHTS ON PEACE

Is the world really moving forward in the direction of peace? Or is it moving in the opposite direction, that of deepening bloodshed and hostility? Everyone worries and agonizes over the question; no one knows the answer.

The midterm elections in America have considerably boosted the fortunes of the Republican Party and dealt a blow to President Johnson and the Democrats. Soviet-American relations seem to be moving in the direction of a gradual easing of tension. On the other hand, as China continues to grow in power and importance, the possibility of a Sino-American conflict increases. The world is entering a new era of strained international relations. When will we ever see the dawning of the day of peace we so fervently long for?

No man who is not completely insane could fail to desire peace. Nothing is so costly and wasteful as war. Until man can find some way to live in peace, he can suffer only loss. How much wealth did the Japanese squander in the Pacific War? And what is far more important than material losses, how many priceless lives were wiped out, what vast resources of human talent were wasted?

And now America is rounding up its young men, the hope of its future, and sending them off to the battlefield to die. Thinking of those young lives, so full of dreams and ambitions, brought to a sudden end— it is almost too pitiful to bear. And the same must of course be said of the Vietnamese youths.

Why must men continue to go to war like this, to keep repeating over and over again the tragedies of history? Everyone cites the same reasons

—conflict of interests, differences of ideology. If not the actual causes, they have certainly been used to lend justification to the wars of the past, to provide a slogan under which hostilities could be pursued.

But in the present day, in view of the existence of nuclear weapons and of man's natural right to survival, it is clear that, regardless of what pretexts may be offered, war itself has become the greatest of all evils.

What I wish to say is that the day when conflicts of interest could be settled by one side seizing something from the other has come to an end. That is an ethic which belongs to a period before man learned how to create through the power of his own wisdom. Values are not something to be snatched away from others but something to be gained through an act of creation. The society that understands nothing but snatching from others is no better than a world of thieves and looters. Its inhabitants, though they wear clothes of the latest fashion, deserve to be called a herd of wild beasts.

In the case of a single family, it is only natural for the family members to cooperate with one another and assist in furthering the family business. If one person gets sick, the family takes care of him, as they do with children. In this way, peace is maintained in the family. Why can't cooperation along the same lines be carried out by the residents of a particular area, or the citizens of a state?

Or, setting our sights still higher, why can't we progress to the point of building an international society in which nations as a whole cooperate with and aid one another? If we could, then I am convinced we would see a truly remarkable progress in the advancement of civilization and the building of a great new society.

In the past, Japan was divided into countless feudal domains. They fought and wrangled with one another. Now they have all been united to form a single nation, the country of Japan. The world today, in the same manner as Japan in the past, is divided up into the various nations of America, the Soviet Union, China, etc. But I believe that, as a matter of historical necessity, the time will come when a world federation that transcends national boundaries will come into being.

With the recent progress in methods of transportation and communication and the dawning of an era of space travel, the conditions needed for the formation of such a federation are already to a large extent fulfilled.

And in fact the inevitability of such a movement has already begun to become apparent in the establishment of such organizations as the EEC. But in order to move from these beginnings to the formation of a world federation that will insure lasting peace, it is necessary to establish the ideal of world nationalism as an ideological foundation for such an organization. In addition, on the practical side, it is imperative that a third force or power emerge in the arena of international politics.

By world nationalism I mean an outlook based upon the firm consciousness that all of mankind constitutes a single corporate body and shares a single fate. At present this sense of a common unity and identity is to be found on the level of national or racial groups. But in the era to come these concepts of national and racial identity must be transcended. Only when the consciousness of all the peoples of the world as a single community is firmly established will true peace, happiness, and prosperity be possible.

And, as I have said, in order to realize this great ideal, to actualize this great philosophy, it is necessary for some powerful third force to appear upon the international scene, one which will be capable of interposing peacefully in the present world of struggle and confrontation and putting an end to its rivalries. I personally would like to believe that Japan is the country destined to fulfill such a role. And as a first step in that direction, it is necessary that Japanese politics be cleansed of their present corruption and malpractice. Only then can Japan hope to achieve international prestige and contribute to the welfare of mankind as a whole.

THE JOY OF MUSIC

My schedule is so busy these days that I almost never have an opportunity to go to a concert. As a result, my musical enjoyment is pretty much confined to listening to records.

The day seldom passes, however, when I don't do at least that. It has become a habit with me over the last twenty years or more. Like a man seeking to slake his thirst in a running stream, when I find a moment of leisure in the quiet of the evening, I sit down and play a record. I don't play it for anyone else to hear, just for myself. If I find a piece I like, I play it over and over again. As you might expect, I've accumulated quite a pile of records with the grooves worn almost smooth.

This habit, which will probably be with me for the rest of my life, goes back to the period just after the war. I was living in a dingy little one-room lodging, and the harshness and desolation of the life around me at times seemed about to destroy me as a human being. No matter how hard I worked each day, no matter what good intentions I had, it looked as though everything I did was bound to end up in failure. It wasn't any simple state of mind easily and conveniently labeled with some technical-sounding term such as spiritual desolation. It was just a feeling that some insane mechanism was consuming all my youthful enthusiasm and energy and turning it into waste and despair. This was the period when I learned how much comfort I could derive from a single phonograph record.

There was much more to listening to records than just enjoying the music. I found that somewhere deep inside my heart I had a musical instrument of my own that would come alive when I listened to a piece

I liked, and even start playing along in harmony with it. Putting on a record was a way of reassuring myself that I still had that musical instrument inside me. That was very important to me, for it gave me a feeling of secret joy. Perhaps it was just the pleasure and satisfaction of knowing I was still a human being. In any event, I learned to get a kind of indescribable enjoyment out of listening to records.

Even now I remember how I used to play Beethoven's Fifth Symphony, the sound filling up the whole narrow room, and how it felt to sit right in the middle of that sound in a kind of daze, listening to it all around me. By the time the fourth movement began, I could hardly stand to go on listening. And when the music ended and I came back to my senses, I could feel a kind of intense exhilaration and courage running through my bloodstream. Before I knew it, it had filled up my whole heart.

It was not long before I wore out my copy of the Fifth Symphony. Another piece that got a great deal of wear in those days was Schumann's song *Zigeunerleben*. When the wild midnight revels of the Gypsies had ended and the song moved on to describe the dawn breaking in the forest, I felt as though all the fatigue and worry had been washed out of my head. Softly, comfortingly, the song spoke to me about the simple joys of living.

I am a very amateur sort of music lover, the kind who knows nothing about musical theory and has never read any of those ponderous books on musical appreciation. In picking out records, I go solely on the basis of whether I like the piece of music or not, simple and naive as that may sound. Pieces I don't like, I have no use for; pieces I do, I never get tired of hearing. As a result, my selections naturally show a certain amount of bias. Others may find bias of this sort reprehensible, but I'm afraid I can't be bothered about their opinions. My tastes probably reflect the rather childish and simple-minded nature I was born with, and if so, there is nothing I can do about them. In a word, when it comes to music, what I care about first of all is being honest and faithful to this inner nature of mine.

I say this because music is something that speaks directly to the heart of man. It needs no intermediary other than sound waves, and has absolutely no use for doctrines, theories, or other such trappings. Furthermore, there is in my opinion no such thing as high class or low class music. It makes no difference to me whether I am listening to a symphony, a concerto, a piece of light music, a folksong, or the latest hit tune, so long as I like it. The same applies to Western versus Oriental music; whichever it is, if it strikes a sympathetic chord in my nature, I like it.

For several years now, I have found myself very much attracted by the works written for the koto by Michio Miyagi. By now a great many of these modern compositions of his have become favorites of mine, including his first work, "Water Transformations," and others such as "The Sound of Rapids," "Spring Sea," "London Rain," "Handball Song," and so on. Late in the evening, before I go to bed, I often lie down in my study and listen to them for an hour or more. At such times I recall with fondness the sounds of the particular type of koto known as a *Taishōgoto*, which I used to hear as a little boy.

Since music is such an important part of my daily life, I never forget to take along a tape recorder and tapes when I go on a trip around Japan or abroad. Travel, and the feelings that go with it, seem to make music even more vivid and moving than at other times. Sometimes the combination of travel and music can stimulate you in a way you would never have expected.

In any event, there is surely nothing more honest and direct than music in revealing man's inner feelings and emotions. Even if it wanted to lie, it would have no way to do so. It employs no words; it never asks that the listener follow a line of reasoning. Certainly it demands nothing so foolish as that the listener strike a solemn pose and try to "understand" it. All one has to do is to open one's ears; then the music within the heart will naturally begin to resound in harmony with the music outside.

This response, this echo within the heart, is to me something to be treasured, for it is proof that human hearts can transcend the barriers of time and space and nationality and converse honestly with one another. Perhaps it could be called the most truly human kind of dialogue men are capable of. Though men may differ in the color of their skin, the language they speak, their customs and ways, or the degree of material culture that surrounds them, it is possible, through the power of music, for them to communicate and respond to each other's innermost feelings.

If, as I believe, the greatest task of mankind as he moves from the twentieth to the twenty-first century is to wipe out once and for all the hostility and bloodshed disfiguring the earth today, then music, which allows men to communicate their inmost feelings to one another, is surely destined to play a major role. It offers the most forceful and effective means by which to set about pursuing that task.

A BOOK

Leaves of Grass—the title itself suggests vigor and irrepressible growth. And indeed the book that bears it overflows with youth, hope, the beauty of nature, and the rhetoric of equality.

When I look at the date on my copy, I see that it was published on May 31, 1949, the translation done by Saika Tomita. I was twenty-one years old in 1949. But I remember that I was around twenty-three when I bought the book at a book store in Kanda, so I must not have purchased it when it first came out. The dust jacket, I recall, was very attractive and had a watercolor of a branch of flowering acacia on it. It was a big thick book—505 pages, I see now as I check. Since it was so soon after the end of the war, most of the books at that time were printed on wretched paper. This, however, was an exception. Printed on high class Japanese paper, it was a very grand and imposing example of bookmaking, especially for that period. I also remember the price, 550 yen, and how I worried at the time about spending so much money. A book like that today would probably cost two or three thousand yen.

What a delicious shock lay in store for me! I remember how profoundly impressed I was by the very first poem, a declaration of the nature of modern man entitled "One's-self I Sing":

> *One's-self I sing, a simple separate person,*
> *Yet utter the word Democratic, the word En-Masse.*
> *Of physiology from top to toe I sing,*
> *Not physiognomy alone nor brain alone is worthy for the*
> *Muse, I say the Form complete is worthier far,*
> *The Female equally with the Male I sing.*

39

To me it seemed to be a hymn to life. There were no ghosts of the past here. The poet's eyes were fixed solely upon the glorious vistas unfolding as the present gives way to the future. It was a prophecy of the birth of a new world, the world of America, and of the coming of a new century. And it was a clear declaration of farewell to the old world, the stolid, weighty world of European civilization.

Walt Whitman cast aside all racial prejudices and broke down all barriers of class. He hated everything in this world that stifles and cramps. He sang the praises of all those who sweat and labor to build the future. And before all else, he sang of himself. The long poem entitled "Song of Myself" with which the 1855 edition of the book opened is an example:

> *I celebrate myself, and sing myself,*
> *And what I assume you shall assume,*
> *For every atom belonging to me as good belongs to you.*

Around the middle of this long poem, we find the following vivid portrait of the poet:

> *Walt Whitman, a kosmos, of Manhattan the son,*
> *Turbulent, fleshy, sensual, eating, drinking and breeding,*
> *No sentimentalist, no stander above men and women or apart*
> *from them,*
> *No more modest than immodest.*

The poet sang of all the countless beings of the new world, describing them just as they appeared to his eyes in the midst of their comings and goings.

How busy it kept him, being the poet of the new world! He could not rest until he had sung of the mountains, the rivers, the seas, even the remote corners of the wilderness and of the city. He sang of all human beings, whether young or old, man or woman, writing of the farmer, the miner, the laborer, of the sailor, the slave, the whore. He sang of the assassinated president and the frustrated revolutionary, the struggling pioneer and the wounded soldier, the wife who had lost a husband, the mother who had lost a son, striving to comfort them and give them courage. He went on to sing of inanimate things, the ship, the machine, the skyscraper.

He was a man of the universe who, believing firmly in the impulse of simple and unclouded love, sang with all his heart in nineteenth century America, so that freedom and equality could be brought to all men, and he went on singing until his death.

In the years following Japan's defeat, when the country was under the occupation forces, I remember with fondness and gratitude what it meant to me, a poor young man, to encounter this collection of poems. And when, in the midst of those gray and troubled times, I learned from that book the secret of how to face the future, my initial admiration gave way to an intense affection. I even memorized a number of the poems that were my particular favorites, and when I was on my way home late at night or at other times, I would often find myself reciting them aloud. One time when I was particularly tired I remember flopping down on the grass in the outer garden of the Meiji Shrine, opening my copy of *Leaves of Grass*, and reading avidly for the better part of an autumn day. Even now there are three yellowed gingko leaves pressed between the pages.

This book was the companion of my youth. No, it would be better to say that this book *was* my youth, for everything that is necessary to youth—courage, passion, the future—I found in it, along with the prayers of the poet.

Pausing to think about the age in which he lived, one realizes that Whitman must have been looked upon as an extremely odd and heretical sort of poet. And yet Emerson, the first person who really appreciated his poetry, was moved to write him a letter in which he praised his poems as "rays of sunlight." I am certainly not the first person who, reading these poems, has had the feeling of a primitive sun whose clear and powerful beams pierce the dense cloud cover to shine upon the earth. These poems have warmed me and given me confidence in the mission I pursue today.

It has been over a hundred years now since this collection of poems first appeared. And yet it is just as Whitman himself said in the poem entitled "So Long!"

> *Camerado, this is no book,*
> *Who touches this touches a man, . . .*

It is a book I will remember all my life.

A MIRROR

I have a mirror. I always keep it with me. Actually, it's nothing more than a piece of broken glass about the size of my palm. The back is covered with little scratches, but that doesn't prevent it from reflecting whatever is put in front of it. A piece of broken mirror, somewhat on the thick side, the kind you could probably find on any trash heap.

It's anything but trash to me. My parents were married in the fourth year of the Taishō era (1915), and my mother as part of her trousseau brought along a mirror stand fitted with a very nice mirror. How many times it must have reflected the face of the young bride, casting back an image clear and undistorted. Twenty years or so later, however, the mirror somehow or other got broken. My eldest brother Kiichi happened to be home at the time, and he and I sorted over the fragments and picked out two of the larger ones to set aside as keepsakes.

Not long after that, the war broke out. My four elder brothers one by one went off to the front, some to fight in China, others in Southeast Asia. My mother, her four oldest sons taken away from her, tried not to show her grief, but she seemed to grow suddenly old. Then the air raids on Tokyo began and soon they were a daily occurrence. I could hardly bear to look at my mother's face. As though it might somehow help to protect her life, I kept the piece of mirror always with me, sticking it carefully inside my shirt as I dodged my way through the incendiary bombs that fell all around us.

Eventually, when the war ended, we received notification that my eldest brother had been killed in the fighting in Burma. I thought at once of the piece of mirror I knew he must have carried in the breast pocket of his uniform. I could imagine him, during a lull in the fighting, taking it out and looking at his unshaven face in it, thinking longingly of his mother at home. I know how he must have felt, because I have a piece of the mirror too, and when I look at it, it brings back memories of my brother.

In the dark and troubled times after Japan's defeat, I left home and moved into lodgings. The room was small, bare, and ugly, but I was too poor to do anything to fix it up. Of course it had no mirror, but fortunately I had my piece of broken mirror with me. I kept it in a drawer of my desk. Every morning before I went to work I would take it out and use it while I examined my skinny face, shaved, combed my hair, and plastered it with pomade to make it stay in place. Once each day, when I held the mirror in my hand, I couldn't help thinking of my mother, even if I hadn't wanted to. Almost unconsciously, I would find myself thinking, Good morning, Mother!

Thinking of his mother once a day—I guess it's the best way for a young man to keep from going wrong. Japanese society at that time was in a state of moral and psychological collapse. Fortunately I managed to avoid falling into the kind of despair and hopelessness that might have led me to do anything self-destructive. I owe it to that battered piece of mirror.

There were times when the mirror told me that the color in my face was not good, that I wasn't looking well. With this as a warning, I would use a few extra rice rationing stamps and get two servings when I went to the lunchroom to eat. There were other times when I stared at my reflection in the mirror, noting the sinister way my cheekbones stuck out, and shuddered with disgust, wondering what I could have done to deserve such an evil-looking face. And at still other times, when I happened to be in a good mood, I would smile to myself in the mirror and break into a soft whistle. In a sense, my mother's care and concern were always with me those days, though they didn't come to me in words. The piece of mirror showed me how I was faring day by day and kept me going on the right path.

When my teacher Jōsei Toda was nineteen years old, he made up his mind to leave the little village in Hokkaido where he had been born and go to Tokyo. At that time his mother gave him an embroidered jacket.

As long as he had the jacket, as long as he wore it when he was working, she told him, he would be able to overcome any difficulties he might encounter. It was white with a dark blue pattern, an intricate embroidery stitched with great care, and all his mother's love and devotion seemed to be stitched in with it. He kept it all his life.

He was imprisoned during the latter years of the war, but in 1945, when the war ended, he was finally released and allowed to return to his home. They say that when he discovered that his house had escaped being burned down in the air raids and that the embroidered jacket was still safe, he told his wife that they need have no more worries. Since the jacket had escaped harm, he knew things would be all right from then on.

An old jacket, a broken mirror, but both of them capable of conveying a mother's prayers. They have a strange power in them that can support and buoy up the human heart when it falters. No doubt many of you will laugh and say, what old-fashioned sentimentality! But to me there is nothing the least bit old-fashioned about the feelings. The jacket and the mirror, they are the only things that have gone out of date.

In 1952, when I married, my wife brought along with her a brand-new mirror stand, and from that time on I looked at my face in the new mirror. One day I came upon my wife with the piece of old mirror in her hand, examining it with a look of puzzlement on her face. She was probably wondering why anyone would keep such a worthless piece of junk around, one which wouldn't even do to amuse a child with. When I saw that the mirror was likely to end up in the trash basket if I didn't speak up, I told my wife about the history attached to it, of the link it formed with my mother and with the brother who had been killed in the war. Somewhere she managed to find a neat little box made of paulownia wood and stored the piece of mirror away in it. The mirror is still safe in its box today.

Even an old fountain pen, if it happened to have belonged to some great writer, is looked on with awe and reverence by the people of later times, for they feel that somehow it is capable of revealing the secrets of the great man's masterpieces.

The piece of broken mirror, whenever I look at it, speaks to me about those hard to describe days of my youth, my mother's prayers, and the sad fate of my eldest brother, and will continue to do so as long as I live.

A PICTURE

I have a picture hanging in my room, a colored reproduction of an etching neatly mounted in a frame. It has been there longer than any of the other pictures on the wall.

I guess it would be difficult to find a more ordinary and undistinguished picture, yet it brings back pleasant memories to me. The picture shows a young girl and young boy talking together in the corner of a room, she looking very sweet and innocent, he with nothing but youth written on his lively, red-cheeked face. Beside the girl is a spinning wheel, the white thread wound around its spindle showing clearly in the picture. The girl is dressed in an old-fashioned style—a long skirt with an apron over it. The boy looks as though he had suddenly remembered something he wanted to say to her and had come dashing into the room. She in turn stares at him with a rapt and charming expression on her face. His cheeks glowing in the light, the boy stands with his supple limbs poised beside her, too engrossed to remember to sit down in the chair behind him. The two are unaware of the aura of youth that surrounds them. Only the eye of the artist has perceived it and, knowing the true beauty and worth of youth, determined to capture it on paper.

This is the kind of picture it is; it seems to overflow with the innocence of youth. At the same time there is not a trace of the affectation, the shyness, the awkward manner of the young. The scene strikes and sustains a pure lyric note, one filled with simple and artless passion. It is this air of innocence and earnest youthfulness that I prize about the picture, and which first drew my attention to it some eight years ago. I have as yet felt no inclination to take it down off the wall.

I acquired the picture at a shop on a certain street in Paris. It was in the fall of 1960, when I was on my first trip to Europe. As I walked along the streets of the city, I had a strange sensation of familiarity, as though I had known them for a long time. Though I knew perfectly well that this was a mere illusion, it made me feel very peculiar. And then, as I was strolling through a park one clear autumn day, I suddenly realized where the illusion came from.

In a sense, I *was* already familiar with these streets and parks from times past. When I was around twenty, I read with enormous enthusiasm Victor Hugo's *Les Misérables*, and the city of Paris, which is the setting for that great novel, had in the course of my reading become quite familiar and well known to me. The illusion that I had actually been in Paris before came solely from awakened memories.

I thought once again of what a splendid work of literature *Les Misérables* is, and the scenes around me seemed more familiar than ever. I turned my head again and again to make certain that I was not missing anything.

I remember coming to a place in front of a park where a number of souvenir shops were lined up, catering to the passing tourists. I stopped in front of a little store that sold prints and paintings. There were seemingly countless pictures hanging inside, nearly all of them reproductions of famous masterpieces. If I'm going to buy reproductions anyway, I thought to myself, it would probably be better to get reproductions of prints or etchings. I therefore picked out four or five, for which I paid, as I recall, the equivalent of around a thousand yen each. One of these is the picture that I now have hanging on my wall.

Because I happened to have *Les Misérables* on my mind at the time, I began to think of the two young people in the picture as Marius, the fighter for liberty, and Cosette, the little orphan girl whom Jean Valjean raised with such loving care. I guess I still think of them that way today.

Les Misérables, Paris, Marius and Cosette—the etching in the frame gathers together a whole train of associations. And it serves as a mirror of my own heart, which until the end of my life will continue to be forever young, will maintain forever the freshness and simplicity of youth.

I believe this because I believe that the eternal splendor of the life force is nothing other than the continuance of youth and simplicity. I will grow old, of course. No one can escape it, even those who at this moment revel in their youth. But I do not want to grow old in spirit. I have no desire to spend the rest of my years hiding behind some pretentious mask of mellowness and maturity, for I know that the essence of the life force, though it manifests itself both as the destructible and the indestructible, is by its nature eternally unchanging.

In the building where I handle the affairs of my organization, there is also a picture hanging on the wall. It is by one of my favorite painters, Kaii Higashiyama. Entitled "Green Pond," it depicts a pond in the midst of a beech forest in Denmark's famous Deer Garden.

I know of no other painter who can equal Higashiyama's wonderful skill in capturing the lyricism inherent in a natural scene. This painting speaks to me quietly yet in a profound manner of the beauty of the life force that lies firmly enfolded within the landscape, and speaks in a way I never tire of. At the hand of the painter, each tree takes on a personality of its own and exudes an air of exhilarating freshness and vitality.

In the thick trunks of the beech trees, in their shrouds of silence, in their dark reflections on the clear green surface of the pond—there just as they stand—they convey in the clearest terms the life force of the trees. At the same time I sense in this landscape painting a dialogue of universal affirmation being carried on between the artist and the natural scene. Warmly, quietly, the picture seems to pulsate with life, as though the inspired heart of the artist were beating away inside it.

When one can grasp the life force that lies enfolded within the characteristics of a particular landscape, it is proof, I believe, that he is possessed of an eloquence that can speak to the universe. The kind of indescribable state of mind known in Buddhist terminology as *Kaiin-zammai* or "Ocean-imprint meditation," in which all truth appears within the Buddha's wisdom just as all things are reflected in the quiet ocean, is perhaps the same sort of thing.

I started out to talk about one picture, but I have ended up talking about two. The fault is not mine, however. This painting of Kaii Higashiyama insisted that it be allowed to take the floor and refused to be put off.

COURAGE,
CONVICTION, AND HOPE

Everyone, I suppose, has memories of his youth. Indeed, if one doesn't, he can hardly be said to have lived his young years at all. I, like everyone else, have my share.

My family was poor, and my four older brothers were all inducted into the army and sent off to the front. As a result, I had neither the money nor the free time to go to school in the ordinary way. Instead I worked during the day, and with the money I made, attended commercial school, and later college, in the evening.

My health was not very good. In spite of that, I tried to do my job the very best way I could. There were times when, running errands for the company I worked for, I had to plod along the Ginza pulling a large cart. Other times I remember having only a single open-collared shirt to wear, even when fall winds had begun to blow. But I didn't feel any sense of shame or embarrassment. Rather I saw myself as a figure in a kind of drama—a youth, smiling, battling the hardships of life—and I even felt a sense of pride. As a matter of fact, I'm certain that the hardships I had to undergo at that time helped to build the foundation for my present way of life.

At that time I had a certain conviction—no, it would be more accurate to call it a resolution. I believed that youth was not something to be lived in vain. I was determined that, poor and shabby as I might be, I would walk with my head held high, taking whatever encouragement I could find and living life to the fullest. This determination, which served to give me strong support at that time, I hold unchanged today. All considerations of position, wealth, and reputation aside, the final victory lies in knowing that one is doing his best as a human being, and it is the greatest kind of victory of all. This is something I intend never to forget until the end of my days.

As I look back over my youth, there are things that give pause for reflection. For one thing, I wish that in my teens and twenties I had done more studying, particularly in basic subjects. I was certainly aware of how important the period of youth is, and I thought I was reading quite a few books. But now I regret that I didn't read ten or twenty times the number that I did. Also, I wish I had done more to train and toughen up my body.

With the aid of hindsight, I realize now how extremely important the period of adolescence really is. Perhaps it would not be too much to say that the whole later course of a person's life is determined by the way in which he passes the years of his youth.

Young people are in the process of building, but for that very reason they are incomplete. They are unknown quantities fraught with limitless possibilities. Young people bring with them the winds of change and reform, and they are the possessors of an enormous and irrepressible vitality. There is little that can equal the greatness of youth. But if a young person should neglect to build and instead spend all his time in idle pursuits, or if he should be overcautious in his goals and allow himself to become weak and ineffectual, then he is guilty, one might say, of committing spiritual suicide. No course of action could be more shallow and ill-considered.

We must realize that every young person who lives is to some extent fired by the youthful passions coursing through his veins. If only firm direction and purpose can be given to these passions, then there is absolutely no doubt that the young can learn to contribute to the welfare of society and to live lives that are truly meaningful. Too many of the leaders of today, however, although quick enough to criticize the young, seem to give little thought to their own failures and shortcomings. They think only of their own fame and profit, work only for their own glory and advancement, and have no understanding at all of the minds and hearts of the young.

This may seem a rather impertinent assertion for me to make. But I would like to mention that, in a piece written ten years ago, I had occasion to observe as follows: "There can be no question that the rise or fall of the nation and the prosperity or decline of the times is in large part determined by the degree of self-awareness that exists on the part of youth and the direction which it takes. . . . There is, however, one fact that must never be overlooked, namely, that whatever constructive efforts youth may engage in, they must invariably be carried out under the inspiration and guidance of the highest of ideals and the ablest of leaders. Without such ideals and such leaders, the passion and vitality of youth, regardless of what age one lives in, will be expended in useless activity. And if the young should be induced to follow false ideologies and leaders, then they will advance in the direction of riot and destruction with the force of an angry torrent."

It is the right of each individual to seek out whatever ideals, whatever philosophy, whatever leaders he wishes. I am saddened only by the fact that the men in political power today seem incapable of offering anything at all to the young. They must, it seems to me, give greater thought and attention to the direction in which they are leading the people of this country. I do not believe that the trend of world developments will permit Japan to continue indefinitely in its present mood of peaceful but irresponsible prosperity.

On the basis of my own experience, I would say that the qualities most vital to youth are courage, conviction, and hope. Courageous action on the part of the young is the source from which all else is created. And it is conviction that guides and lends support to courage. Looking at society today, how many countless people do we see who lack conviction! A life devoted solely to flattering others and chiming in with their views is as empty and worthless as foam upon a wave. Conviction knows no faltering or hesitation, no confusion of aims. And this kind of conviction is something that grows up naturally out of one's actual efforts to fulfill one's responsibilities and mission in life. Finally, a life that is without hope, a young person who feels he has no future, is little more than a living corpse. The greatest men of all are those whose youthful years are full of dreams and ideals, and who continue throughout their lives to pursue their dreams and ideals.

Young people are the treasures of the nation, the wealth of the age to come. There is no power to compare with the value of this treasure. To do anything that would jeopardize the future of these young people or deprive them of their vigor is equivalent to casting one's treasures into the sea. And those leaders who would actually go a step further and send the young onto the battlefield, where precious lives are lost forever —surely they deserve to be called the most evil of men.

I have a great fondness for the young, and my greatest delight is to watch them grow. The sight of them maturing in an atmosphere of wisdom, peace, and happiness makes my heart leap with joy. It is my present hope that I may spend the rest of my life walking side by side with the young and breathing the air they breathe. And if I may in time live to see them ascend the platform we have built together and soar aloft one by one in the cause of world peace and cultural advancement, I will know the fulfillment of my hopes, the attainment of my greatest joy.

NEVER LET LIFE GET
THE BETTER OF YOU

If I had not had Jōsei Toda for my teacher, I would never have amount-
ed to anything at all. It took me a long time to realize this fact. While
Toda Sensei was still alive, I was completely wrapped up in the struggle
for survival, and during the ten years following his death, I have devoted
every ounce of my energy to the task of carrying on and enlarging the
work which he began. But now, as I look back upon all that has happened
in the past twenty years and consider in a dispassionate manner what has
been accomplished so far, I can see that everything has turned out just
as Toda Sensei predicted it would on the various occasions when he
talked to me and others about our future. He also told us about events
to come in the much more distant future.

My first meeting with him took place on a hot summer night in 1947,
when I was nineteen years old. Tokyo, like the rest of Japan, was under
the control of the occupation forces. At that time, the entire area south
of the Imperial Palace was little more than a burned-out plain. Only here
and there in the desolate night could one see dim lights flickering in the
little makeshift shacks erected on the ruins, or in the air raid shelters that
served as living quarters for many.

My family lived in the area and made a living by growing and gathering certain edible seaweed known as *nori*. We somehow managed to
keep the business going during the war and in the years following it,
though on a much reduced scale. (Of my four older brothers, the eldest
had been reported killed in action and the others had not yet been repatri-
ated from overseas.) In the midst of poverty and want, Japanese society
was undergoing profound changes. The cry of democracy was heard on

52

every street corner; the old powers and figures of authority one after another faltered and crumbled.

For persons of my generation, who had had nationalism and absolute obedience to the Emperor drummed into them from the time they were old enough to understand anything, it seemed as though everything we had believed had suddenly been reduced to naught. We young people had nothing whatever to trust and believe in. It is hardly surprising that we found our bodies and minds tormented day after day by a sense of fretfulness and apprehension.

It was under such conditions that, almost as a matter of natural impulse, two or three of us got together in a group to exchange books. Starved for something to read, we treasured whatever volumes we could find that had escaped being burned in the air raids, and fell on them hungrily. Novels, works of philosophy, biographies of great men, books on science —we devoured anything and everything that came to hand and then shared our impressions with one another. But although we would have endless debates on the significance of what we had read, when we faced the harsh realities of the times, the spiritual support and confidence we thought we had gained from our reading would suddenly melt away.

In addition to this group, I had another friend from elementary school days who from time to time came to visit me. One day she invited me to attend a meeting, to be held at her house, on "The Philosophy of the Life Force." It was then that I first heard the name Jōsei Toda.

Purely out of motives of curiosity, I decided to go, and took along with me the other members of the reading group.

We found ourselves being addressed by a man in his forties with a somewhat hoarse voice and a relaxed manner. His thick glasses caught the light, and I remember being particularly impressed by his broad, prominent forehead. At first I didn't understand anything he was saying, though I gathered it had to do with Buddhist doctrine. I had no sooner come to that conclusion, however, than I noticed that his discussion was also interspersed with acute observations on the political situation and other matters pertaining to everyday life. But just as I would begin to follow what he was saying, he would suddenly come out with a string of difficult-sounding Buddhist terms. In all, my impression was that of a very strange and unfamiliar philosophy.

Still, his remarks did not sound like the usual sermon of a religious leader, nor, for that matter, like what one would call a conventional lecture on philosophy. They seemed to be very concrete and to the point, without any bandying about of abstract ideas and concepts, and at the same time they appeared to suggest that the plain and simple facts of everyday life were in themselves capable of embodying the highest kinds of truth. The room was filled to overflowing with middle-aged men, housewives, young girls, and sturdy-looking young men. All of them kept their eyes fixed on Toda Sensei and listened with rapt attention. Though all were shabbily dressed, I knew that they were good, law-abiding people. And there seemed to be about these simple people an undefinable aura of life and vitality.

Toda Sensei did not strike me as belonging to any type of personality that I was familiar with. He had a brusque way of speaking, but also conveyed a sense of unlimited warmth. As I stared intently at him, our lines of vision would sometimes meet. At such times, I would drop my eyes in confusion, but when I would look up again after a moment, I felt as though his gaze were still fixed upon me. It sounds like an odd thing to say, but in the course of the talk I somehow began to feel I had known him for a long time.

At the end of the talk, my friend introduced me to him. "Well, well," he said, his eyes shining behind the thick lenses as he looked for a moment squarely into my face. Then, as though he had understood something, he broke into a warm smile.

"How old are you?" he asked.

With that sense of having known him before, I answered without hesitation, "Nineteen."

"Nineteen, you say?" He seemed to have remembered something. "I was nineteen when I came to Tokyo. I came from Hokkaido, a country hick on my first visit to the big city."

I remember that he was chewing on a Jintan tablet, a kind of breath sweetener, and smoking a cigarette at the same time. I felt an impulse to take the opportunity to ask him about some of the doubts I had concerning life and society. What is the right kind of life? What does true patriotism mean? What do you think of the emperor system? What is Buddhism really all about?

I did ask him, and his replies were direct and without equivocation. He appeared to be answering without the slightest difficulty, but that in fact, I now know, was simply an indication of how rapidly his mind worked. Without any trace of awkwardness or evasion, he addressed himself directly to the very heart of each question. I came away fully satisfied with his answers, realizing for the first time in my life that truth was after all something very close at hand.

On August 24, just ten days after that evening with Toda Sensei, I became a follower of the Nichiren Shōshū and a member of the Sōka Gakkai. Little by little I came to understand the true aptness and worth of Buddhist philosophy, and to appreciate what a rare kind of person Jōsei Toda was. Meanwhile, I continued to work during the day and to go to school in the evenings. But I had already begun to have doubts about this way of life, and about a year later, following what seemed to be the most natural course of events, I made up my mind to quit my job and go to work for the publishing company that Toda Sensei headed.

That was in January, 1949. It was very hard work. The postwar Japanese economy, just recovering from the effects of defeat, was tossed about like a boat on the surging waves of inflation. A modest enterprise like Toda Sensei's, needless to say, could not escape being buffeted and battered in the harsh economic climate. From the end of 1949 until the summer of 1951 the battle for survival was fought on a daily basis.

One by one the employees of the company left and went elsewhere, until I was the only person remaining to deal with our creditors. The deterioration of my health and my general frustration at life had both reached the danger point, and yet I made no move to leave Toda Sensei. On the contrary, at some point I made up my mind that I would stick with him regardless of what happened, even though it might mean following him to the depths of hell. I believed in him, I believed in the rightness of the Buddhist teachings of Nichiren Daishōnin, and I was determined to stick by them and continue the fight just as long as possible.

"I have failed in business, but I have not failed in my life and I have not failed in my Buddhism!" In uttering these words, Toda Sensei showed that he was fully aware of his mission. This was something I sensed very strongly. From that point onward, everything was a matter of rebuilding.

In order to help Toda Sensei to rebuild his business and the Sōka Gakkai, it became necessary for me to give up my schooling. Sensei was sorry that, as his only disciple, I had to take this step. "From now on," he said, "I'll teach you everything!"

From that time on, for the next several years, I received private instruction from Toda Sensei at his home or early in the morning at his office. Law, political science, economics, chemistry, astronomy, classical Chinese—with the utmost care he taught me almost every conceivable subject, except foreign languages. It seemed as though he was determined to pass on to me every bit of learning that he himself possessed.

His own learning he had acquired largely through his own efforts. After finishing elementary school in Hokkaido, he became an apprentice to a tradesman, simultaneously studying on his own until he had qualified himself as an assistant elementary school teacher. He then took a job as a teacher in a coal-mining region in Yūbari, and in time became a regular teacher. At the age of nineteen he came to Tokyo, where he happened to become acquainted with Tsunesaburō Makiguchi, the man who was to be his leader and teacher for the rest of his life. He attended middle school classes at night and eventually passed the examination certifying that he had completed the equivalent of four years of middle school training. Later he studied at Chūō University.

As you can see, he was to a large degree self-educated. Schools were something which he needed not to acquire learning but to give certification to the learning he had already gained. He was especially versed in the field of mathematics and for a time operated a very successful private school called the Jishū Gakkan. Also, under the name Jōgai Toda, he wrote a book entitled *Guide to Arithmetic*, which was much used by students reviewing for exams and which sold over a million copies, making it one of the best sellers of the time. I expect that many of those who were students in those days remember the book with fondness.

In addition to the various subjects already mentioned, Toda Sensei also gave me instruction, and this with great intensity and enthusiasm, in the life force philosophy of Buddhism. And as he passed on to me detailed explanations of the Buddhist scriptures and the writings of Nichiren Daishōnin, he drew my attention to the ways in which these teachings relate to various modern systems of thought. I have subsequently come to realize that, in addition to this formal instruction, the efforts which he was putting forward to rebuild the Sōka Gakkai, and in fact every aspect of his daily life, were in a sense a form of teaching, earnestly given and of inestimable value.

I in turn responded to this intense and challenging training with the best I could muster in the way of diligence and endurance. I tried to absorb everything he had to give me, though I fell short of his expectations so often that, almost until the day of his death, I was subject to frequent scoldings.

Reflecting on my life leaves me with a sense of wonder and awe at just how much Toda Sensei's existence has meant to me. That a man so mediocre as myself could succeed the late Toda Sensei as head of the Sōka Gakkai and assist in the unprecedented undertaking of *kōsen rufu*, the propagation of the spirit and teachings of true Buddhism, is due solely to the fact that I have never for so much as an instant let the image of this great leader depart from my mind and heart. The greatest happiness of my life is that I was able to meet him and become his disciple and follower, and that the relationship of teacher and student was sustained until the very end of his life.

HOW I SPENT
MY YOUTH

Memories of youth stir me with their boundless fascination. There were fearful storms and blinding rains, but there were also days of sunshine spent in beautiful gardens.

At times I find myself so drawn to the memories of the past that I forget everything else just to wander in the world of my youth. And at such times I ask myself reprovingly if I couldn't have lived a little better kind of life.

For me, those years were shadowed by war. I was seventeen when the war ended. Because of the tubercular condition of my lungs, I had left the munitions factory where I had earlier been assigned to work, and was resting at home. Around May of 1945 I began getting my belongings together in preparation for a move to the country which, it was hoped, would help my condition. But just at that time there was a large-scale air raid on Tokyo, and my belongings, our house, and everything else burned up. The future looked completely black for me.

How hateful war is! Regardless of what excuses men may offer, they must once and for all cease this senseless killing. On the very first page of my novel, *The Human Revolution*, I wrote: "Nothing is so cruel as war. Nothing is so tragic as war." These are words that have been etched deeply and indelibly on my heart ever since those bitter days.

How different the area of Tokyo where my home was situated looks today! By the end of the war, it had been reduced to a charred plain, hardly a building left standing. Now an express highway has been built through the area, the monorail passes through it on its way to the airport, and the new super-express train runs close by. At the same time, rows of factories have sprung up, blackening the air with smoke from their chimneys and pouring their polluted wastes into the waters of Tokyo Bay. The bay itself has been extensively filled in, so that now the shoreline is far from where it used to be.

In the old days there was a bathing beach at Ōmori, near our house, and the shore was famous as a place for growing the edible seaweed called *nori*. Now, needless to say, one would not dream of bathing in the water. The people who used to make a living growing *nori* have all moved elsewhere. Nothing remains of the place as it once was.

I hear there is a movement afoot to build a museum to preserve examples of the tools and other equipment used in the old *nori* industry. It makes one take notice of the fearful rapidity with which the world changes. And yet, although we speak of this or that having changed, these are in most cases merely superficial changes, transformations in the outward form of things. It is much too soon to conclude that anything so basic as the human heart and mind have changed.

Comparing the life of the young people of today with my own right after the war, I find vast differences. Still, I cannot believe that there have been any great changes in the fundamental way of life of the young. And I also think that, in spite of the harshness of the times, those of us who were young right after the war had a youth that was as essentially "youthful" as any being lived today.

What are the distinctive characteristics of youth? Vitality, passions that race like a mountain torrent, dreams so vast they have no end, the purity and innocence of snow. Youth is the flower of human life, a pearl above price.

Regardless of who the person may be or what era he happens to live in, the way in which he spends his youth will in large part determine the course of the rest of his life. The span of youth is relatively brief. If during this period one should do anything that might endanger his future, he would in effect be gambling away his most valuable possession.

A rich man is reported to have said, "If I could only relive my youth, I would gladly give my whole fortune in exchange." And Anatole France, in his usual witty manner, is said to have remarked, "If I had been the Creator, I would have arranged it so that youth came at the end of life!"

As I look back over my own youth, I feel like calling out to the young people of today and begging them to live their youth in a way that will leave them with no regrets. There are, of course, a thousand different ways to live one's life. I do not for a moment mean that everyone should conform to a single pattern; that would be much too dull and confining. What I do wish to say is that whatever direction one may choose to advance, he must never cease to think about his personal growth and development as a human being. If the process of growth should ever come to an end, then, although one may still be in the years of youth, his heart will already have become old.

During my younger years, if I found myself with any free time, I always tried to spend it reading. In those days right after the war, of course, books were very hard to come by. I remember making a special trip to the Iwanami Book Store and standing in line for a considerable time just to buy one book. As a result, each book I was able to lay my hands on was a thing of great value to me. Reading these books was both a pleasure and a challenge.

Although I was battling at the time with a protracted illness and the hardships of daily life, I vowed in my heart not only that I would never neglect my reading, but also that I would continue to pursue it for the rest of my life.

My teacher always used to say to me and his other followers, "You young people must set aside some spare time for reading and speculation."

Again and again you hear people say, I don't have the time to read! It's not that they haven't the time. What is lacking is the necessary composure of mind and heart. But anyone who allows himself to be completely dominated by his work or his environment is being negligent about his personal growth and maturity.

If young people, particularly the young people of today, do not do as much reading as they ought to, they will find that their intellect will become rusted, their critical powers will falter, and their future will be permanently darkened.

Reading is not an occupation or pastime of one particular group in society only. Whether one is a tradesman, a factory worker, or an office worker, it is perfectly natural to read in order to keep up with what is going on and enlarge one's knowledge. Moreover, it is nothing that demands that a person be in a particular environment or frame of mind.

The important thing is to make reading a regular part of one's daily activities, bit by bit building up a foundation of knowledge. If one reads no more than twenty minutes each day, think how much learning and culture can be acquired in the course of a year!

However, it is very important to choose the books one is to read with care. The books I would like to see people read are the one's that delve deeply into the problems of human life and the proper way of living, books of real quality which have been read and admired by the men and women of the past and have stood the test of time.

A person's true worth is not determined by the amount of formal education he has had, his position in society, his reputation, or his wealth. When all of these have been set aside, it is the actual ability of the individual, his character, and the care and intensity with which he works constantly to improve himself that are the determining factors.

The more ineffectual and lacking in ability a person may be, the more attention he will pay to outward show, the more he will try to hide his lack of worth behind a mask of pretension. No life could be more bitter, more foolish, and more tragic than that of such a person, nor at times more laughable. The important thing is not to be in too great a hurry, not to tire, but little by little to work constructively and in one's own way to further one's growth and maturity.

In addition to reading, I was extremely fond of music when I was young, and in fact I still am. Beethoven's Fifth Symphony was a particular favorite of mine.

Goethe said that listening to the Fifth Symphony made him feel as though the ceiling were spinning around. And a famous Russian writer observed that it filled him with a feeling of courage.

I too have listened to that symphony many times when I was tired or had to face some particularly difficult situation. At such times, I would feel a sense of courage arising within me and filling my whole body, and I would say to myself with determination, All right, I won't let it get me down! I'll keep on as long as I have any strength left!

When I listen intently to a quiet piece of music, I am reminded of the depth and immense broadness of the ocean. The experience allows me to view the various problems of everyday life with a certain calmness and detachment and to face the future unperturbed.

If the music is lively and dramatic, I find myself stirred with passions flaming like the sun, and at times I am seized by the impulse to leap into action on the spot. I cannot help thinking that music is imbued with all the rhythms of the universe, that it is capable of expressing all the aspects of human life.

No matter how intense the pressure of daily affairs, I hope I will always have the leisure to listen to music. Or perhaps it would be more appropriate to say that, the more intense the pressure of affairs, the more I look to music to provide me with new courage, with fresh vision and unlimited strength.

I believe that not only music but other kinds of hobbies and interests are of vital importance in life. A person who is without hobbies is somehow narrow and colorless in personality. On the other hand, of course, it is absurd to become so engrossed in one's hobbies that one neglects his work or endangers his source of livelihood.

Young people do not live in the past. But they do not live only in the present either; they live in the future as well. There is no doubt what the American poet Longfellow meant when he advised that one should never look to the past, but should trust to the present and greet the future bravely. And the philosopher Karl Hilty has said, "Life must be an unending progress. Up until the very last instant, each day should be an act of creation." When I first heard these inspired words of the poet and the philosopher, I was profoundly stirred. They were like great waves washing over my heart, and I resolved to do my utmost to live my youthful years in accordance with them.

Youth is a time of hardships, but it is also a time when the light of hope streams in. The person who grows up with an ever constant hope in the future is the true singer of youth's song. As Schiller said, "As long as the sun shines, hope too shall shine!"

No matter what hardships and illness I suffered in my youth, no matter how precarious the fate of the Japanese nation seemed to be, the sun always shone for me. Somewhere in the depths of my heart there were seeds of hope which, no matter how often they were trampled on or pressed down, insisted upon growing. Or perhaps hope is not the seeds but the sun which shines within the heart of each person.

OVERCOMING HARDSHIP

On the long voyage of life, there are times when the sun shines with the warmth and brightness of a day in spring. And there are other times, like bitter winter nights, when one must battle the freezing cold. Periods of hardship, we might say, are the winter nights of life.

Some people encounter their worst hardships during their youth and then, having successfully overcome them, go on to live in relative ease and happiness for the rest of their days. There are others who succeed in avoiding hardship during their youth, only to have it descend upon them in old age.

In my case, I tried to experience what hardships I could in my youth, hoping that in the process of overcoming them I could build a firm foundation for later life. I do not mean that I had the slightest intention of going out of my way to invite unusual hardship or to become any different from an ordinary human being. Even now I realize that there are an untold number of people in the world who have struggled, and continue to struggle, against far greater difficulties than I.

But, because I had my share of sickness and poverty and other such worries, I am able in full measure to sympathize with others who are sick or troubled. It is something I am deeply thankful for.

The American poet Whitman said something to the effect that the more one has shivered in the cold, the better he can appreciate the warmth of the sun, and the more troubles he has experienced in the world, the better he can understand the true value of human life.

And indeed winter never lasts forever. After the bitter struggles of winter is bound to come the sunshine of spring.

The important thing is never to give in to hardship. In time of trial, one must learn to endure whatever may come, and thereby strengthen and improve oneself. After all, it is only the person who has experienced the cold of winter who can truly savor and enjoy with his whole being the warm sunshine of spring.

"The star that governs your destiny is in your own heart," one poet has said. There can be no doubt of it. Whatever one's circumstances, whatever one's past, the star of destiny, the forces that determine one's future, are nowhere but in the heart and the mind of the individual.

Regardless of what storms may blow, what angry waves may threaten, you must keep shining at all times with a pure and steady light. This is what I want to say to all the young people of today who are undergoing hardship, for, depending upon how you bear up under hardship, the trials of today could turn out to be your most precious possession.

As I have mentioned elsewhere, I had four elder brothers. Since all four were called into military service during the war, I was left with many of the tasks and responsibilities that under ordinary circumstances would have been theirs. Our house was burned down in the air raids, and though my parents both worked as hard as they could and tried not to burden their children with hardship, I naturally had to look out to some extent for my younger brothers and my little sister.

Moreover, I was at that time suffering from tuberculosis of the lungs, and much of my strength was consumed simply in the battle with that disease. In any ordinary family today, a person in the condition I was in would as a matter of course be sent to a sanatorium for an extended period of treatment and rest. But in the years I am speaking about, toward the end of the war and just after it, such a step was out of the question.

Every day was a struggle for me. Toward evening, the low fever symptomatic of the disease would invariably come on. And then there was the cough, which never let up. How many times, even after I had gone to bed, it persisted, tormenting me so that I could hardly get to sleep.

The doctor at one point said I would probably not last much past twenty-three or twenty-four. After I went to work at the company headed by my teacher Jōsei Toda, my health continued to be a constant source of worry, and on one occasion he confided to my parents that he did not think I would live to see thirty. But I kept on day after day doing

64

the best I could to carry out my job, strenuous though it was. I don't mean by this to sound as though I am advising anyone to do anything foolish or to deliberately put an undue strain on his health. But as I look back at my own case, I have a feeling that if I hadn't had the daily challenge of my job before me, my body might well have succumbed to the disease. Because I knew in my mind that I had a job to do, both my body and my spirit rose to the challenge, and eventually I was able to regain my health.

As Cervantes, the author of *Don Quixote*, said, "Where there's life, there's hope." There were many times when my condition was so bad that I lost all courage and was on the point of resigning myself to death. But then I would say to myself, I'm still alive, which means there is still hope! And I would resolve to go on fighting.

I know there must be any number of people in the world today who are much sicker than I was. I would appeal to such people to face their trials with a firm and undespairing heart and to determine never to surrender in their battle with disease.

This applies not only to the case of illness. No matter what kind of difficult situations one finds oneself in, some opportunity, some opening, can always be found to fight one's way out of them. The important thing is always to have hope and to face the future bravely.

But to return to my own story, I went to work for my teacher Toda Sensei in January of 1949, when I was twenty-one. My job was editing a magazine, and for someone in my physical condition, it was hard work. But, as I have already implied, the fact that I had the work to challenge me each day turned out in fact to be a blessing.

I was also receiving intensive instruction and training from Toda Sensei in a number of different subjects. Sometimes I would find myself being scolded with a fury like that of a hundred thunderbolts striking all at once, while at other times he would show infinite gentleness and patience. I never had the slightest doubt that at heart he had deep faith in me, and that behind the scoldings was his loving concern and desire to make me into a person of real worth, capable of doing any kind of work. For this reason it was a boundless joy to be able to work for him, and I never for a moment thought of giving up merely because of the tough and exacting training I was subjected to.

A truly warm human relationship—how much in the way of hope and courage and conviction it is capable of giving! It is not too much to say that in the end everything I have today I owe to the fact that I was able to encounter such a great teacher, one who was willing to trust me without question.

To be looked upon as trustworthy and reliable is surely one of the most valuable assets a man can have, regardless of his occupation. And for a young person, to be trusted in his work is of prime importance. If a young person does not learn to inspire trust in others, he is almost certain to end up a failure.

At present, they say, we are living in the age of irresponsibility, and certainly there is a tendency for people to not only disregard but to be completely indifferent to the trust which others put in them. But so long as human society exists, it is patent that trustworthiness will continue to be of basic importance, and anyone who betrays his trust will become a social outcast, one for whom nothing but defeat can lie in store. Today he may flaunt his irresponsible manner with complacency; in the end he will come to nothing but grief.

I believe it was the Japanese novelist Saneatsu Mushanokōji who said, "One word from a person who is qualified to be trusted carries more weight than ten thousand words from someone who is not."

Trust is hard to build up and easy to destroy. Trust that one has spent ten years in nurturing can be wiped out in an instant by some little slip-up in word or action. A pretentious and overconfident manner which tries to hide the lack of real ability will quickly be shown up when a time of crisis arises. The person who works with all his might to carry out his mission is the one who in the end will win the trust of those around him. The type of man I truly respect is one who, though he may be doing a rather inconspicuous and unexciting job, still does it conscientiously, advancing step by step and patiently working to improve himself.

When I speak of the importance of inspiring trust, however, I do not mean that one should be constantly attentive simply to choosing the safest course and succeeding at all cost. For a young person, this is a fatal error. On the contrary, the mistakes of one's young years are often far more important than we could ever guess in helping to build a foundation for the future. Therefore I would like to see young people do each day's work with courage, aware that they still have much to learn, but determined to do the best they can.

The English novelist Goldsmith remarked that his greatest boast was not that he had never known failure, but that each time he fell down, he picked himself up again.

I have forgotten the author, but the following words also come to mind, words that have always moved me deeply. "Failure—what is failure? Is it not a constant occurrence in the world? And is it not the ladder to great accomplishment? Because of it, we gain a kind of experience that we could never acquire from ten thousand books. . . . Ah! Failure is the means by which Heaven bestows happiness upon us. In truth, it is the greatest treasure of life!"

To lose heart just because of one or two failures is the height of foolishness. Life is a long, long journey. The truly sad thing is not to fail in youth, but to live a highly successful and prosperous life and then, when one is well along in years, to encounter sudden misfortune or failure.

In youth one should go forward with courage, understanding that the more often one fails, the firmer will be the foundation which one builds for his future life and happiness.

In addition, it is necessary for young people to have the fearlessness to recognize their failures as failures and honestly take responsibility for them. This kind of attitude I find most admirable in young people. Above all, one must avoid the opposite tendency, which refuses to recognize one's own responsibility and in a cowardly manner tries to shift the blame to others.

Finally, one must have the breadth of mind to consider the source of one's failures and in a cool and objective manner to judge how and where one went wrong. For such judgment will serve as the source of future value creation.

The sight of a young person striving to reach the goal he has set for himself is one of the most powerful, most refreshing, most beautiful things in the world. Nowhere in the world is there a beauty to match that of a young person who has fought with and overcome hardship.

ON STAYING YOUNG
AND SIMPLE IN HEART

The great German poet Schiller wrote the following words: "Youth may face the world in nakedness. For with the purity of youth, the inspiration of youth, the health, the frankness, the vigor with which it shines, the hope with which it burns, it possesses far more than the greatest statesman or general."

If I were to sum up in a few words my beliefs concerning the kind of life I want to lead, I would say that I hope always to retain the sincerity of youth, to be an unfailing friend and supporter of the common people, and to spend my life among them.

Perhaps it is just part of my nature as a native born Tokyoite, but I hate any kind of concealment or pretense, any kind of covering up of the truth. In fact, I am so open about things that I have at times received complaints or friendly bits of advice from the persons around me. But I have never tried to change my ways, and in fact, I don't think I could change this trait even if I wanted to.

In the end, I think people are happiest when they are living the kind of life that accords with their true nature. As soon as they try to pretend, to put on airs and be something they aren't, then immediately a host of difficulties begin to arise. No matter how high the office or position a person may hold, no matter how much fame and glory he enjoys, if he has to keep up some kind of show or pretense, he will never know true happiness in his heart.

I believe it was Montaigne who said, "There is nothing more beautiful in the world than the beauty of a woman, and yet women themselves prize artifice and think of nothing but their makeup."

Women, I presume, consider a certain amount of makeup a necessary part of their personal adornment. But to go beyond that necessary amount and smear on a lot of gaudy cosmetics is simply to expend effort on making oneself look ugly.

To try to put on too much show, to try to make yourself look grander than you really are, is surely not in any way a failing confined to women. Men show the same tendency, though the particular ways in which it is manifested differ from women's ways. Indeed, men are probably even more susceptible than women to this failing.

In any event, I would like to paraphrase the words of Montaigne and state my opinion: There is nothing more beautiful in the world than the beauty of a human being, and yet human beings themselves prize artifice and think of nothing but their makeup.

Human beings just as they are—when they are ugly, there is nothing uglier. But when human nature is sincere and beautiful, there is no more beautiful thing to be found.

The great English statesman Disraeli once said, "There is no wisdom greater than sincerity." For us Japanese, who are so troubled by the problem of insincere politicians, such words coming from the mouth of a political leader may strike us as very strange. Nevertheless, I agree completely with the sentiment.

I am fortunate in being able to have a great many friends both in Japan and abroad, friends who are of all different races and all different classes in society. And in the course of forming these friendships, what has impressed me most deeply is the fact that the strongest, most beautiful, and most valuable type of human relationship is one which dispenses with all show and pretense and allows two people to come together in complete frankness and openness.

No matter how strong the hostility another person may feel toward you, if you approach him in an attitude of complete sincerity and truth, he will invariably abandon his ill will and respond with friendliness. Even when dealing with foreigners who do not understand your language, you will find that a sense of sincerity is the one thing that somehow in a very subtle way gets across to others. Perhaps human beings possess some deep inner power that allows them to sense sincerity instinctively. In any event, the degree to which they can do so is almost frightening.

69

If all men had warm heart-to-heart relationships, then how could they ever bring themselves to hate and kill one another? Though I have on numerous occasions issued a call for world peace or world federation, I know that in the end the problem can only be solved on the level of the individual human being and through the formation of the kind of relationships I have described.

I look upon myself as one of the common people and their unfailing ally and friend. I lived according to this belief and fought for it in the past, and I am determined from now until my death to continue to be the friend of the weak and the implacable enemy of violence and of hypocrisy in government. I believe that true democracy must have as its foundation the happiness of the common people, who make up the majority of the citizens of Japan.

In the old days in Japan it was customary to employ such adjectives as "vulgar," "crude," or "coarse" when speaking of the common people. Such a manner of speaking, of course, merely reflects the prejudices of the nobility and the members of the warrior class, who themselves in many cases had lower class origins. In the present age of democracy, anyone continuing to hold such prejudiced views can only be described as a victim of anachronistic and completely muddled thinking.

I myself was born the son of a commoner family, grew up among the common people, and consider myself very fortunate for it. As a result, I have a boundless love and affection for the common people, and take the greatest possible pride in living with the common people and fighting on their behalf.

Although we are supposed to be living in an age of democracy, I wonder if the common people are not being compelled, as in the past, to undergo sacrifice. In the meanwhile, the Japanese government, which fails to represent the interests of the citizens as a whole, falls into a state of decay and rottenness and begins to emit a putrid odor. And in the field of economics as well, although the country, by favoring large-scale enterprises, has achieved an impressive rate of growth, it has been gained at the expense of incalculable sacrifice on the part of the common people.

Must the interests of the common people, who make up 80 or 90 percent of the population, be sacrificed in order to benefit a privileged class comprising only 10 or 20 percent of the population, that of the capitalists and politicians?

I say this fully realizing that, beyond the right to vote and the other basic human rights guaranteed to me by the Constitution, I have no more power or authority than any other member of the common people. As a class we are weak; there can be no doubt of that. But if one stops to think of it, the highest skyscraper can stand only so long as the ground beneath it continues to support it. In the same way, men of high position and extensive power, such as the statesmen and generals mentioned by Schiller, can only exercise their authority so long as they have the support of the common people.

Regarded in this fashion, we would have to say that the common people ought to possess the greatest power of all. The common people are the real mothers and masters, while the men who exercise authority in the world are in fact no more than their sons and servants. Perhaps herein lies the true meaning of democracy and the principle of the sovereignty of the people.

Although Japan is ostensibly a democratic state, the Japanese people even today in their hearts seem to feel that politicians and bureaucrats belong to some special group above the common level. It is a way of thinking which they appear unable to rid themselves of.

The so-called black mist scandals, charges of corruption and payoffs that recently shook the political and financial worlds in Japan, had their ultimate origin in this same kind of misconception about the nature and locus of power.

In any event, it is up to us to create with our own hands a new era, an era of true democracy. We must do it for our own sake, if for no other reason.

For the sake of the young people who must live in and bear responsibility for the future era to come, I believe that we must do our very best, at least within our own respective fields of endeavor, to build a brighter and more upright society. It is a task that demands all we have to give.

I have described in another essay how my own life was completely changed at the age of nineteen as a result of my encounter with Jōsei Toda, the great man who was to become my teacher. Because of this meeting, I was able to pass the years of my youth under his guidance, and as a result I am convinced that I deserve to be considered one of the most fortunate persons in the world. Even now I feel his teachings, alive and full of vitality, within my heart.

One of the things he taught me is that "we must see to it that the word *misery* is wiped out of existence!" And on another occasion I recall him saying, "In the final analysis, the greatest kind of man is one who can go through life without ever losing the faith and passion of his youthful years." Although that goal may be no more than an ideal, I too want to try to live in such a way as to remain young and simple in heart. And I want to live a life that knows no stagnation, but which constantly moves forward and upward.

I have heard of a certain principal of an elementary school who, when he was over sixty, began to study English intensively. I am also told that in England and other countries it is not uncommon for persons who are well along in years to go back to college in order to continue their education.

There are a vast number of people who, in order to remain faithful to their beliefs and to live the kind of lives they believe to be right, have overcome numerous hardships and gone on with courage and confidence until they attained their goal. When I think of their example, I realize that I myself am still young, both in body and spirit.

My youth is of the most ordinary kind. And it involves constantly talking with young people and working with them.

I respect young people above all others. Why? Because it is young people who act as the support of the present age, and who in the future will formulate the ideals and direct the movements of the world.

I often try to lend encouragement to the young people under me, telling them that "youth is another name for the period of building." By "building," I mean working for the completion and happiness of the individual, and at the same time working toward the building of a better society.

And while I encourage others with these words, I try to give a careful ear to them myself.

THE POINT WHERE
HOME AND SOCIETY MEET

My teacher Jōsei Toda often used to give this advice to housewives: "Don't ever quarrel with your husband in the morning when he is setting off for work. If a man has angry words with his wife when he is leaving the house, his mood will be ruined for the whole day and he won't be able to do a good day's work. Riding the train, he will feel grumpy; even if he tries to read a magazine he will continue to feel grumpy, and whatever intentions he had of putting in a hard day's work will be brought to nothing. So make certain that you send him off to work with a smile and a cheerful 'goodbye,' even if you have to force yourself to do it!"

The moment when a man stands at the door ready to leave for work is the point at which the home and society as a whole touch. If some kind of trouble or impairment should occur at this vital point of contact, then the free exchange of ideas and impulses that should flow between the home and society will be impeded. The lifeblood of the family will be cut off, as it were, and it will begin to suffer anemia.

Now as I think of it, I realize how right my teacher was in pointing out the importance of this. If a man has gone away from the house in a bad mood in the morning, his mood will not improve even after the day's work is completed. On the contrary, as evening approaches he will recall more vividly the events of the morning and his wife's ugly face (however she may look in reality, he will undoubtedly think of her as ugly).

In a mood of anger and spite, he may well decide to have a drink instead of going straight home, and there will be no lack of bad companions on hand to encourage him. Likely as not he will seek solace with another husband suffering from the same complaint and they will keep

73

each other company, going from place to place drinking and not getting home until late in the night.

The wife, meanwhile, has probably been in much the same kind of mood as her husband. She watched the television but it didn't interest her; she did the washing but it didn't take her mind off the incidents of the morning. And when evening comes, she sits waiting for her husband, becoming more irritable and angry as the hours pass. When the husband finally arrives, you may be certain that will not be the end of the matter.

The next morning, both husband and wife will start off the day in bad humor, and the same scene will be repeated. This is a vicious cycle that is not only senseless but can be highly damaging to the peace of the family. If it is allowed to continue, it may well lead to tragic consequences for the marriage.

When we look back, we see that it all began with one moment of ill temper that took place in the morning. As a result of that, the whole atmosphere of the home becomes changed. And children, who are extremely sensitive to such things, will not fail to notice the change.

I am careful never to quarrel with my wife in front of the children. I remember my parents quarreling one time when I was of elementary school age. Just the sight of it made me feel miserable and upset. On top of that, a good friend of mine happened to come by just at that moment, so that to my original distress was added the shame and embarrassment of having him see what was going on. Even now, some thirty years later, I can remember vividly how wretched I felt. Anyone who stops to consider the scar such incidents may leave upon the innocent minds of children will certainly take care never to quarrel in front of them.

The moment when the husband returns home in the evening is perhaps even more crucial than the one when he leaves in the morning. What are the first words of greeting as he comes in the door? Does he hear something like, "Why are you so late? Did you stop somewhere on the way?" Or does he hear, "I'll bet you're tired. Dinner's all ready." I leave the reader to decide which greeting is more likely to buoy up the husband's spirits and make him feel that it's all worth doing.

Any woman who hopes to be a good wife and mother will be especially careful about these two moments in the morning and the evening, for they are crucial to the happiness of the home.

74

A MOTHER'S LOVE

My mother, whose name is Ichi, was born in the twenty-eighth year of the Meiji era (1895) and hence is now close to eighty. She lives a quiet life in the suburbs of Tokyo.

She raised eight children of her own and adopted and raised two other children from outside. Now that her sons have families of their own and her only daughter has also married, she can boast a total of thirteen grandchildren.

She is a very simple woman without any education, but she succeeded in raising all of her children in good health. It always pleases me to think that, in its own way, her life represents a victorious one.

Her life has by no means been entirely happy, at least in her early years. My father Nenokichi, who died in 1956, was so hardheaded and obstinate that he was known among his relatives and neighbors as "Mr. Stubborn." I am certain it must have required enormous patience on my mother's part to have stuck with him until the end of his life.

When I was a child our home was at Ōmori, on the edge of the bay in the southern part of Tokyo. My mother did her share of the work—growing and gathering *nori*—laboring in a way that it would be difficult for an ordinary city housewife of today to imagine. Even now I can picture her, a little woman, in the dead of winter getting up before the dawn and working away until late in the evening, not even stopping to rest when she had caught a cold.

As far as the education of her children was concerned, she didn't seem to have any special ambitions. I never remember her saying a single word that would incite us to dream of success in the future or make us feel that

75

the acquiring of degrees and formal education was an important or desirable thing.

For all her lack of pretension, I do recall her cautioning us again and again never to tell lies or do anything to cause trouble to other people. I am grateful to her that she did, for once I got out into the world I realized that these after all were the most important things for us to have learned.

A woman who never put on airs of any kind, her whole happiness lay in seeing her children grow up in good health, and she was willing to do any amount of work to achieve that goal. That's the kind of mother she was; I can't imagine any other kind that I would rather have.

During those years of nightmare and tragedy during the Pacific War, our family suffered the same as everyone else. My four elder brothers, who had just grown to maturity and reached the age where they could relieve my mother of some of the work, were one after another called up for military service, summoned, it was said, for the sake of the Emperor and the sake of the nation. My mother, true to the spirit demanded of the mothers of a nation at war, never shed a single tear. She sent each of her sons off to foreign lands with a smile on her face. I wonder, though, what was in her heart at that time.

One thing in particular I admired about my mother was the fact that, in spite of the large number of children she had to cope with, she was always completely fair in her treatment of them. In everything, from the dividing up of food to the settling of quarrels, she showed fairness and impartiality. Intervening in the numerous fights that arose among us children, she would always take care to determine just who was in the right and who wasn't, and would settle the matter in a way that left everyone satisfied. She was in fact a highly skilled judge and arbitrator.

Since I was the weakest and most sickly among all the boys, I naturally caused her the most care and worry. After the war, when I was going to school at night, she would always wait up for me, no matter how late I came home. Then she would heat up a bowl of noodles for me, saying, "I'll bet you had a hard day!" In that one sentence, which she would repeat over and over, I could sense the boundless tenderness of a mother's love.

No matter how old I get, she still treats me like a child. If she has any

76

occasion to give me a present, it is always cigarettes, accompanied with the admonition not to smoke too much. Her presents mean more to me than any others, because they convey to me a feeling of simple and profound love.

Thinking of what my mother has meant to me, I always feel sorry for children who have lost their mothers. Their whole childhood must be darkened by the loss in ways that it is impossible to measure. No one can take a mother's place. That is why I always tell young mothers that they must take care of themselves and make certain that they stay in good health. If only for the sake of the children, it is imperative that they do so.

You often used to hear people say, "Women are weak but mothers are strong." Nowadays one almost tends to think that the opposite has become true. Right after the war it was for a time fashionable to remark that women and silk stockings had both grown much stronger than in the past. Certainly women have gained many new rights in recent years, including legal equality with men and the right to vote. But these various rights in themselves do not necessarily contribute to the inner satisfaction or growth of women. On the contrary, it would almost seem that women these days have become weaker and less able to perform the specifically feminine roles and duties assigned them by society. One finds mothers, for example, who are incapable of raising even one child in a satisfactory manner, which would seem to indicate a truly lamentable loss of spirit.

Nothing is as strong as a mother's love. And it is precisely through the medium of motherly love that the true strength of the female sex is preserved and carried on. Regardless of how strong a woman may be in other ways, if she is incapable of managing her responsibilities as a mother, then one can only say that she has lost her true femininity.

During the feudal period in Japan, when the position of women was extremely low and the male head of the family had absolute power over its members, it was motherhood that gave women the strength to endure hardship and abuse. Though a young wife might be teased and tormented by her mother-in-law and sisters-in-law, she knew that there was nothing she could do but bear it. Her fortitude was no doubt aided and sustained by the love she felt for her children. She knew that she must carry on for the sake of her children.

77

The women of the Meiji period, in the latter part of the preceding century and the first part of the present one, continued in many cases to receive the kind of strict upbringing characteristic of the samurai class, which placed great emphasis upon family honor. In other cases, where they happened to be members of merchant families, they often displayed considerable economic wisdom and directed the management of the entire household. But regardless of other roles, their primary one was that of a mother, and that was the source of their real strength.

In the following Taishō period, which lasted from 1912 to 1925, new currents of freedom and democracy began to stir in Japan. Women were finally freed from restrictive bonds, and the era of the modern woman began. In spite of certain changes and innovations, however, many of the old traditions and customs of the past remained in effect, and Confucian ethical concepts continued as before to serve as the basis for social standards.

And what is the situation in the postwar years? We find that both the old family system and the former system of Confucian values have collapsed completely. What is more, nothing that would serve to take their place has appeared. Perhaps this is the reason that even the instincts of motherly love seem to falter so frequently these days.

I by no means wish to sound as though I am praising the old family system, with its large number of individuals living under one roof and its strong paternalism. Modern society has awakened a sense of self-awareness in people and made them conscious of their existence as individuals. In view of the times, these changes would appear to be a matter of historical necessity and they deserve to be recognized and accepted. And I also believe that it is inevitable in the future that the individual rather than the family will increasingly become the basic unit in society. There has been a dramatic increase in the number of newlyweds who set up housekeeping for themselves, and we have probably already entered the age when the basic pattern will be for such young couples to create a new family environment and formulate new ideals and ways of life.

Before we carelessly discard the traditions which formed the basis of the old family system, I wonder if we ought not to consider whether there are elements worth being carried on and incorporated into the new way of life. After all, the inheritance one receives from one's parents is not confined to material goods alone. The traditions and techniques of daily life handed down from the past constitute an important heritage for the people of the nation as a whole. And among these customs, which have remained vital over a period of so many years, there are many which lend beauty and meaning to daily life, and deserve to be perpetuated. After all any new culture of real value must invariably be founded to some extent upon the traditions of the past.

In the old days, the mother-in-law would carefully teach the young bride the proper way to cook vegetables and prepare pickles, and these efforts not only contributed to the health and economy of the household but at the same time created a warm atmosphere of family solidarity. The hands of the typical Meiji period mother, I have no doubt, smelled of the fermenting rice-bran in which the pickles were made. In this way the wife helped to economize on household expenses and turned out nourishing and tasty meals.

Nowadays in most homes everything in the meal, from the main dish to the pickles, comes out of a plastic package or is whipped up from some ready-made preparation. As a result, daily life for the housewife has certainly become much more convenient and less tiring, but what means is left now for her to create a distinctive family atmosphere all her own or to give expression to her love as a wife and mother? I believe it is a question we ought to think long and hard about.

When motherhood ceases to be meaningful to a woman, to that extent she loses her identity as a human being. Surely this is something that I am not alone in worrying about.

A WORD
TO YOUNG MOTHERS

What is a mother? The sun that lights up the family, the earth on which it stands. She possesses the power to bring forth and nurture life, a power greater and more to be respected than any in the world. She is the heart of the home, the star performer, the queen of the realm.

Raichō Hiratsuka, one of the first women in Japan to work for the advancement and emancipation of women, has declared that "in the beginning, women *were* the sun!" Even now, it seems to me, as well as in the near future, and for all time, we may say that, for each individual life in its beginning stages, the mother is in fact the sun to it.

For children, the mother is a unique symbol of safety and absolute trustworthiness. Her warm, love-filled breast is a fountain of endless life and vitality.

When a child comes home from school in the afternoon and hears his mother's words of greeting, what joy it is to him, what a source of courage and self-confidence. Though the child may have gotten wet in the rain, been blown about by the wind, be shivering with cold or even have been beaten in some game or bruised in a rough-and-tumble fight, once he comes into contact with the warmth and vitality of his mother, his physical and mental hurts and pains will be healed and he will be ready to go forth again the next day, walking firmly and with confidence to meet whatever lies ahead.

The influence of the mother on the child is like the air around him, invisible but absolute in its power and importance. It may even be said that, as a place for the training and education of the child, the home is of greater importance than the school. It is a common mistake these days to suppose that schools are the only place where education takes place. It is this kind of mistaken thinking that has led to the scramble on the part of parents to get their children into the best schools, and has caused people to forget what real education is all about.

If one sets out to trace the causes leading children into delinquency, one will invariably find that there is a lack of warm human relationships in the home. It is my contention that the home must be a place in which one can relax amid an atmosphere of abundant warmth and love, and that when it is, it can serve as the most important training ground for the child.

Above all, the actions of the parents serve as a model for the child. The mind of a child is sensitive and acute, and will invariably reflect the attitudes and the way of life of the parents. A clever child will at times deliberately pretend not to notice things. If he lives in a home where the way of life is irregular or dissolute, he may appear to be completely absorbed in his studies or wrapped up in play. But if one takes this to mean that he has not noticed what is going on around him or that he is uninfluenced by it, one would be highly mistaken.

Sometimes something will make such a vivid impression on a child's mind and remain so deeply engraved in its depths that it will warp his entire character, inflicting a psychological injury that is almost impossible to cure and which will remain with him for the rest of his life.

On the other hand, the image of parents who are tender and affectionate with the child and with one another will likewise make a strong impression on the child's mind, and will invariably serve as a source of moral support to him in the future if he should be tempted to follow evil ways or should lose confidence in himself. Like a lamp, it will lead him along the path he should go.

In the postwar period in Japan, rapid social changes have caused the nature of the family to change in countless ways. With families in which the grandparents live with the children and grandchildren becoming increasingly few, we have entered the age of the nuclear family. The old system of the extended family with its paternalism and authoritarianism is undergoing basic changes.

Some people go so far as to refer to this process as the collapse of the family system. I prefer, however, to regard it as a process of change rather than of collapse. After all, the family system, which has lasted for at least several thousand years, is hardly likely to collapse and disappear as rapidly as all that.

The old type of family system, the old ways of living, can no longer be carried on just as they were in the past. But the kind of family that can meet the needs of postwar society in Japan will in some sense, it seems to me, be a more important and vital institution than the family of prewar times. The question facing young wives and mothers today is how they can best adapt to these new conditions in society and arrange family life in the wisest and most efficient manner so that the husband remains healthy and satisfied and the educational needs of the children are met. It is this kind of wisdom that the new era we are living in demands.

Fortunately, the young mothers of today have been educated during the postwar era and know what democracy and a democratic type of education are. They are thus in a much happier position than the members of the older generation, who were brought up before the war and have no understanding or experience of democratic education. Seeing only that the old ideals of the past have crumbled and decayed, they are left with a feeling of uncertainty about the future and a loss of confidence in themselves.

For younger mothers, it is a time to join with their children in breathing the new air around them and building a new century. But to evolve a new kind of home life, it is necessary to have new ideals. The old secretive and clannish ways, which kept one family shut off from another, are no longer appropriate. Moreover, the old ways of thinking, which placed all emphasis upon the advancement and worldly success of the family members, too often led to a loss of true humanity and are not in keeping with the present changing times.

I believe that the new family of the future must function in a free and open manner and be oriented toward society as a whole. It must above all respect the individualism of the child, be rich in creativity and a sense of social responsibility, and cultivate in the hearts of its members a reverence toward life, a belief in equality, and a longing for peace.

Recently we have heard much about the problem of the so-called educational mamas, mothers who are overly concerned about the proper education of their children. Discussions have brought out many of the factors contributing to the problem, such as an exaggerated concern over exactly what type of school a child attends, or a dissatisfaction with the quality of education being given in the public schools. But if we center our examination of the problem on the mothers themselves, we will find that in most cases the trouble stems from the fact that they are attempting to use their children as a means to give expression to their own vanity and pride.

One often encounters such mothers, nagging their children to study harder, insisting that they take private lessons in the piano, painting, or some other subject, trying with all their might to force the child into some preconceived mold that they consider desirable. It is not a pretty sight. Needless to say, they run a grave risk of destroying the individuality of the child entirely.

One can certainly understand the mother's desire to do all she can for her child. But is it really the wishes and needs of the child she is thinking of when she does these things, or is it her own? In many instances, it is very difficult to tell.

One professor of educational theory has written of the problem in these words: "If the mother, consciously or unconsciously, continues to consider not the child's dreams but her own, not the child's happiness but her own, as the point of departure in planning for his education, the result will be something as artificial as the dwarfed trees in a *bonsai*. The child, who wants only to spread his wings and soar into the sky by his own power, is completely deprived of his freedom. He ends up like a bird in a cage. These may sound like very strong words, but I do not believe they amount to an exaggeration."

While I would agree with this view entirely, I also believe that, if we examine these excessively busy and ambitious mothers more closely, we will find that the cause of their behavior lies in a basically mistaken view of human nature.

Anyone with intelligence and sensitivity is bound to recognize that all occupations in life are basically equal, and that there is no such thing as an intrinsically exalted or lowly occupation. If one were to search for some basis on which to discriminate among them, I would say it lies not in the occupation itself but in the attitude of the person pursuing it, that an attitude or approach to life characterized by artificiality is to be abhorred, and one which is characterized by complete sincerity and a striving to do the very best within one's capacity is the most admirable. This outlook accords with the principles of democracy and is the only one, I believe, that is constructive, practical, and correct.

It is the responsibility of the mother to teach the child the proper attitude and way of life, one which is marked by sincerity and a respect for true human values. The mother who thinks only of getting her child into the right school, of his entering a lucrative profession, and teaches him to live a life of pretense and artificiality, though she would seem to be expending all her zeal in working for the happiness of her child, is in fact condemning him to a life of unhappiness as a human being.

Regarding the question of the ethical training of the young, one often hears criticism leveled at the schools because of the lack of proper relationships between the teachers and the students. Of course the relationship between teacher and student should be one of warmth and trust. But before the mothers hasten to place all the blame on the teacher, I hope they will stop to reflect once more and ask themselves if they have done everything *they* should have done for their children.

I'm sure many mothers at this point will be tempted to reply, "I'm doing the best I can!" I have no intention of denying that. I only question whether they are in fact respecting the individualism of their children, and doing all they should to encourage a true spirit of creativity in the child and a sense of social grace and responsibility. Have they in fact created the kind of home atmosphere in which the family members can feel completely at ease and free to express themselves as human beings, from which they can draw new strength, and in which the children can observe and acquire the proper attitudes toward life? This is what I would urge the mothers of today to ask themselves, turning the question over seriously in their minds and attempting to answer it in a spirit of complete honesty.

The person who exercises the greatest influence in forming a child's character, teaching him ethical standards, and giving him a sense of decency and honesty is of course none other than the mother. This should be a source of great pride for her; at the same time, it should inspire her with a strong feeling of responsibility.

This fact is too often overlooked, it seems to me. As a result, mothers feel that if only they can get their child into a good school, he will automatically turn out to be a person of brilliance and fine character. And when they drive the child to study beyond his capacity until his individuality and creativity have become blighted and withered, then they try to shift the responsibility onto the shoulders of the school.

Life does not consist simply of studying in school. The period after school has ended in the afternoon, when the child is playing with his neighborhood friends, can be of equal importance in the learning process, teaching him invaluable lessons in how to get along with others. Play itself, especially when it is varied in nature, serves in an important way to foster creativity in the child.

From the child's point of view, every person he comes into contact with is a teacher of sorts, and every activity he engages in teaches him something about life. A wise mother will realize this and make it her duty to see that the child is given proper guidance, allowed to develop his own individuality at a leisurely pace, and provided with a broad and varied education.

I have three children of my own, and I am trying to see that they are raised in as free and relaxed a manner as possible. Children have their own dreams. The things they learn in the process of pursuing and struggling to realize those dreams will become a part of their very blood and physical being, far more meaningful to them than learning forced upon them from outside.

To sum up, I would stress that mothers must try, through the medium of love and care, to teach their children to live the kind of life which shows true respect for the human being. They should teach their children that, in terms of the basic nature of a human being, such things as titles, position, and wealth are no more than superficial trimmings. And when I speak of teaching, I do not necessarily mean giving instruction in words. Even without the medium of words, the mother's outlook upon life will naturally be communicated to the child and exercise an influence upon him. This wordless teaching, which conveys to the child the correct attitude toward life, will help him to grow into the kind of self-reliant adult needed in a democratic society. I am certain I am not alone in looking forward to the time when these young people will work together to build the bright world of the future, or in believing firmly that they have the power to do it.

In a sense, therefore, it is the mothers who are in a position to play the most important role in helping to realize this future age of happiness and peace. That is why I call upon them to have confidence, to face the future with hope, and to make of themselves living examples of the proper attitude and approach to life.

GOOD AND EVIL

In an essay in another series, in which I discussed the French writer André Malraux, I mentioned his intention of joining the Bengali Liberation Army. It is impossible to determine exactly what he had in mind, since the intervention of the Indian Army has made possible the establishment of the state of Bangladesh. Once more, as in the east-west division of Germany and the north-south division of Korea, fragmentation has led to the creation of one more state in the world, a process all too frequent in recent years and one which it seems impossible to reverse.

The plight of the countless refugees who fled from East Pakistan to India was pitiful to contemplate; no less pitiful were those people in the liberated areas who, accused of aiding the enemy, ended up being the target of merciless revenge. The Bihari tribes, in spite of their desperate pleas for help, were subjected to the sternest kind of repression by the citizens of the new state.

From the infamous guillotine of the French Revolution to the purges carried out in the wake of the Russian Revolution, revenge and oppression seem always to have been a part of every revolutionary upheaval in human history. As though to give vent to their rage, men who in the past have been oppressed resort to acts of cruelty and violence when they find themselves in a position of power. In attempting to avenge wrongs by committing even greater wrongs, human beings seem to be caught in a pitiful and unending cycle of hatred and retaliation from which they are powerless to break away. Animals, we are told, will prey upon their own kind only when faced with imminent starvation. Human beings, by contrast, kill out of motives of passion, greed, ideology, or merely for the sport of it. In human conflicts, each side is convinced that it is absolutely right and its opponent absolutely wrong. And this conviction of right is proclaimed loudly to lend justification both to the cruelty of the oppressor and the vengeance of the oppressed. How tragic, to think that in this world there should exist a concept of "justice" that countenances the taking of human life!

When we look at the history of warfare, we see that both parties in the conflict invariably hold this conviction—justice is with them alone, their own nation is wholly good and their adversary the epitome of evil. A classic example is the militaristic government in power in Japan during the Pacific War, which railed at the "Anglo-American devils." But in fact is it ever possible to discriminate so clearly between good and evil?

I recall a short story I once read about how a group of good men banded together to carry out a revolution. In the world at present, they reasoned, it is always the evil men who wield power and oppress the good. Only when the truly good men of the world seize power can there be lasting peace. They then proceeded to carry out their revolution and massacre every one of the evil men. Their actions throughout were based upon the lofty justification that, since they themselves were good, they would be incapable of committing any wickedness. In order to build a society made up entirely of good men, it was *of course* necessary to eliminate all evil men. The story ended on a note of intense irony, however, for it left the reader wondering if this band of virtuous conspirators had not, at some point in the proceedings, turned into an organization of the most evil and depraved kind.

The well-known Meiji period novelist Natsume Sōseki, in his work entitled *Kokoro* or *The Heart*, takes up this question of whether men in the end can really be labeled "good" or "evil." In the final letter which Sensei writes to the protagonist of the novel before committing suicide, he says, "I wonder if you still remember what I told you about there being no innately bad men in the world. I also told you that you must be constantly on guard, because so many of the good men will, if the occasion should arise, suddenly turn into bad men." In this penetrating passage, Sōseki touches upon one of the riddles of the human heart, the fact that so often it is the most virtuous man who turns into the greatest scoundrel.

Buddhist philosophy, in explaining the nature of life, employs the concept of the Ten Realms or states of existence. According to this concept, the various conditions under which life exists can be divided into ten stages. The lowest is that known as hell, the highest that of the Buddha, while the realm of humanity, in which one lives as a human being, exists exactly midway between these two extremes. Initially, man stands in a morally central or neutral position, but hidden within him as possible directions in which the life force may develop are the potentialities to become either very good or very evil. This doctrine, it seems to me, sheds a profound light upon the nature of the life force that underlies all existence.

Good and evil, Heaven and Hell, saint and sinner—in the West these concepts have been regarded as dualisms whose terms are opposite and mutually exclusive. This type of thinking is manifested most clearly perhaps in the writings of St. Augustine through the opposing concepts of spirit and flesh. The spirit is the eternal path and leads one to God, the flesh the path at the end of which lie only darkness and destruction. Accordingly, man can hope for salvation only if he casts off the things of the flesh and devotes himself wholly to the things of the spirit.

Such thinking implies a simple paradigm: spirit equals goodness and flesh equals evil. But so long as good and evil are seen as opposites and the spirit and the body are viewed dualistically, then man will always be faced with the necessity of choosing one over the other.

Though one may assert that the flesh is evil, the fact is that as living human beings we depend upon it to survive, to move, and to think. If the flesh is so evil we must cast it aside and pursue only the things of the spirit, then we are faced with a task which is patently impossible to accomplish so long as we remain alive. From this arises the conclusion that man cannot hope to attain perfect goodness during his life on earth, and must wait for the life after death before such hopes can be fulfilled. He must wait, in other words, for the kingdom of Heaven. And if he does not believe in Heaven, or in his capability of attaining it, he is left with nothing but the hell of his present human existence, a situation which all too often drives him into the clutches of nihilism.

Even today, in places where this type of thinking prevails, one finds on the one hand men who practice the most extreme austerity and asceticism in their search for the good, and on the other hand those who give themselves up to complete hedonism and nihilism.

In my opinion, it is a mistake to view good and evil as mutually exclusive entities. Man is a complex being. He embraces within a single unified personality the elements of both good and evil. And through the light of pure and unclouded wisdom, he must somehow come to understand this fact, to comprehend his true nature. Once this has been accomplished, we will no longer have "good" men who suddenly turn into scoundrels, or men who, in their pursuit of goodness, force themselves and others into acts of hypocrisy.

The same thing, I believe, may be said of the ego, which in the present age is so often regarded as the source of major evil in man. The ego itself is not evil, though it has the potentiality for evil, just as it has the potentiality for good. If the ego were in fact evil, then we would be faced with the same dilemma as that in the concept of the inherent evilness of the flesh. As long as man remains alive, he would continue to be the embodiment of evil, with no hope ever of escaping from that fate.

The problem, in my view, is how this ego, which has the potentiality to become either good or evil, can best be guided and utilized. To solve this, we must first have a clear grasp of the true nature of the ego. In other words, we must come to understand once and for all the life force which exists within us. It seems to me an important sign of progress that, in view of the impasse which modern civilization faces, men's attention is now beginning to be focused upon just that problem—the understanding of the ego which lies at the heart of human existence.

By directing our attention to the understanding of the ego, we will be able, I believe, to rid ourselves of the arrogance of the past, and to guide human wisdom and passion and will power in the direction of goodness. This should be our task for the turbulent year ahead.

THE THROB OF LIFE

I love to talk with people. When the schedule of a busy day is over, nothing is more pleasant than sitting around in a relaxed mood and chatting with people I know well. At such times there is of course no fixed topic of discussion and the conversation may touch upon any number of subjects—art, science, society, the life of man in general. These conversations provide me with many new facts and fresh insights, and I find them an invaluable source of intellectual stimulation. Thus it has become a practice of mine to meet with as many different kinds of persons as possible and to exchange views with them on a wide variety of topics.

During an informal gathering a few evenings ago, I learned of the following piece of news from the scientific world, which concerns the return to life of some microorganisms that are two hundred and fifty million years old. Word of the event, which came from Moscow, was reported in a brief thirty-line article tucked away in a corner of the newspaper. It said that these organisms had flourished in the ocean during the Permian period, the last part of the Paleozoic era. Entrapped in a crystal of potassium ore, they had lain dormant for all these millions of years, but in a test tube they came to life once more.

The Permian period occurred over two hundred million years in the past. It was a time when the *tibolita* and *fusulina* swam through the great seas, and reptiles and amphibians had just begun to make their appearance on land. It was a forerunner of the famous age of the dinosaurs, but needless to say was eons before the time when man, or his ancestors, the anthropoid apes, made their appearance on earth.

The microbes were recovered from the region of the Ural Mountains, which during this ancient period was under the sea. Somehow they became trapped in the potassium and remained there, locked in peaceful slumber. While incalculable myriads of other creatures flourished and passed into extinction and age after age of the world's history unfolded, these tiny sparks of life, which look to the eye like faint dots of red, remained in their dormant state. And yet now, awakened from their long sleep, they have returned to life in the test tube and have begun to multiply with startling vigor.

Hearing the story, I could not help being astounded at the tenacity of the life force inherent in such simple beings. Inside the inanimate ore, they were cut off from air, warmth, water, nourishment—every element needed to sustain life. Under such circumstances, they had no choice but to lie dormant like pieces of lifeless matter. But at the same time the ore served as a perfect resting place and guardian for these tiny bits of slumbering life. If modern science had not rescued them, they might have gone on sleeping for hundreds of millions, even for billions, of years more. And yet their slumber was such that, once the proper conditions were brought to bear on it, it would immediately give way to a vigorous and pulsing vitality and the breath of life would resume. It was a peaceful rest and one which never ceased to contain within it the potentiality for activity.

Some twenty years ago in Japan we read of the "Lotuses of Ōga," two-thousand-year-old lotus seeds, found at a place called Ōga, which when watered and cared for, proceeded to sprout and bloom. The plants grown from these seeds continue to flourish, we are told, and have been sent to various research laboratories throughout the country. This news startled the world by proving that the seeds of plants can preserve their potentiality for growth over remarkably long periods of time.

But whether it be the lotus seeds of Ōga or the microorganisms from the Ural Mountains, we can only be amazed by the ability of these tiny life forms to spring back to vigor and activity after having existed for so long in a state seemingly inanimate and devoid of the spark of life. That recent evening, as I turned over in my mind these scattered thoughts on the mystery of life, I could not help feeling that even the stillness of the night that enveloped me was somehow pulsing with a hidden vitality.

According to one theory, there are in the vastness of the universe several hundred million stars, and they possess the same conditions to support life as we have on earth. It is only reasonable to suppose, therefore, that creatures resembling man exist on at least some of them. It is even possible, with the advanced knowledge of modern astronomy, to surmise that beings inhabiting other planets possess an intelligence equal or even superior to that of man. It is only the vast distances separating us that have so far prevented any communication between our planet and theirs. I wonder if they too suffer the same kind of miseries that plague human life, if they too are caught up in an endless cycle of internecine struggles? Or have they, perhaps, learned how to respect life, and fashioned for themselves a green paradise in which to dwell?

Scientists now surmise that it is possible for life to exist under conditions far harsher than those prevailing on earth. For example, even in an environment of fifty degrees below zero centigrade, ammonia may take the place of water in sustaining some form of life. And at the opposite extreme, in an environment of several hundred degrees above zero, sulfur may replace water and substances such as silicon take on the characteristics of a living organism.

Silicon, as it happens, is an ingredient of rocks. If silicon can indeed turn into a living organism, I am at a loss to imagine what sort of thoughts it might have. In any event, we can only be filled with wonder at the fortitude of the life force manifesting itself in such incredibly hot or cold environments, environments in which we would not think it possible to exist. Once more we must voice our amazement at the mystery of life.

The year before last, in a meteor which had fallen to earth out of some unknown corner of the universe, scientists discovered an amino acid distinctively different from any known on earth. The discovery attracted great attention, for it offered the first clear proof that at least the basis for life exists outside our planet. When we think that such amino acids, which have the power to initiate life, are floating about in the near vacuum of outer space, it almost seems as though the universe itself is a giant womb, fertile in all its corners with the seeds of life.

The French philosopher Henri Bergson (1859–1941) in his work *Creative Evolution* expounded a striking metaphysical system in which the entire universe was conceived of as a process of evolution. When I was in my late teens I became fascinated with Bergson's philosophy. Even now his key term *élan vital* remains vivid in my mind. In a sense, the term is the cry arising from the soul of the philosopher as he glimpsed the mystery of life and the universe.

He describes in the following words his state of mind when he finished writing *Creative Evolution*: "In the past I was extremely interested in mathematics and physics. I would not have hesitated to say that matter constituted the central mystery. But later all that changed. Once I had begun to focus my attention on the life force, I realized that it was the true mystery."

We men and women of modern times, it seems to me, need to listen humbly and with an open mind to the words of this "philosopher of life." For so long as we continue aimlessly to expend the life force within us and fail to apply our minds to the mystery of life and the universe, we are being unfaithful both to ourselves and to the universe.

We are told that the Pioneer 10 probe, which was launched recently to explore Jupiter, carries a message addressed to the men of space. It may be millions of years before the message reaches anyone, but it is good to know that we can dream of such a time. The constellations adorning the heavens appear to move impassively along their respective orbits, yet at the same time they are throbbing with a vital and dynamic rhythm. I want to live the kind of life that allows me the leisure to converse each evening with the universe and to ponder humbly upon the mystery of the life force and the purposiveness embodied therein. For somewhere, I believe, lies the unseen foundation upon which man's true humanity must rest.

TO LIVE

Over half a year has passed since I began writing a series of essays. When I wrote the first one, the autumn leaves were at their height, dying the surface of the streams with their brilliant hues. Then before we knew it the leaves fell and we were in the grip of winter. That too passed. The frozen ground began to warm again, and horsetails poked up their impertinent faces to tell us spring was on the way. The cherries, lords of the spring, proudly displayed their profusion of petals, but now their blossoms have all scattered and the trees are garbed in thick foliage.

When the appropriate season comes, each tree and plant steps forward to perform its brief dance, making the most of the time allotted it; then it moves aside to make way for the next performer. While human beings wear out their days struggling through a tangle of worries and complications, nature goes blithely and unhindered on her way, setting her own pace, following her own rhythms, never deviating from her accustomed course.

All the movements of nature are governed by time, and man, no less than the plants and trees, is subject to the same harsh master. No matter how man may boast of being the lord of creation or try to force his will upon other living beings, he too is fated to change and grow old along with the inexorable flow of time. How meaningless and futile is it for him, then, to lose his composure over some trifling annoyance and to end up hating, cheating, even killing his fellow man!

In terms of biological development, if the entire period from the formation of the earth down to the present were to be regarded as constituting a single day, then the interval encompassing the history of mankind would be about two minutes in duration. By the history of mankind I mean the entire span of time from the appearance of the anthropoid apes down through the age when men began to use tools, the beginnings of higher culture in Egypt and India, the Greek and Roman periods, the Middle Ages, and so on to the present.

And astronomically speaking—that is, in terms of the formation of the universe as a whole—this arduously wrought span of human history would last barely the space of a second.

As one scholar put it, man and the other beings inhabiting the surface of the earth are, when viewed in relation to the vastness of the universe, no more than swarms of insignificant insects. The same scholar asserts that no matter how men may discourse on lofty principles and labor to create their culture, they are in fact, like particles of matter in a liquid, merely going through the random motions of the Brownian movement. In a way, I suppose, he is right. Thinking only in terms of a purely mechanistic materialism, it is not surprising that human beings should appear this way. But if man is indeed so lowly a being, then it is more important than ever that he should consider how to live his life in such a way as to give the clearest proof of his humanity.

In a sense, it is correct to say that man's life is predetermined, dependent as it is upon the larger rhythms of nature and the universe. Both his freedom of movement and his capabilities are severely limited. The secret of human life is to discover how, within these limitations, one can create values that are unlimited.

Though man may appear to be no more than an insect, his thought is capable of embracing the entire universe. While his lifetime may seem no longer than a moment in duration, his thought enables him to range at will through the infinite past and the infinite future. And if this is so, then even the life of a single individual ought to be capable of embodying the infinity of space and time. It is both man's right and his duty to ask what the purpose of human life is, for only in the act of doing so can he truly fulfill himself as a human being.

> "The fifty years of man's life, when measured against the world, seem a mere dream, a phantom. Is there anything born that does not in time perish?"

96

The famous military dictator Oda Nobunaga (1534–82), who helped to unify Japan and rescue it from chaos, was fond of reciting this passage. Born into the turbulent world of the Warring States period, his life unfolded like a stirring drama, reaching its stormy conclusion at the age of forty-nine when he was struck down by an assassin.

Since Nobunaga's time the average life span has been considerably extended. Now we should probably speak of "the seventy years of man's life." But from the point of view of the endless flow of time, it remains a dream or a phantom, something brief and fleeting. Each man must decide how to spend this brief lifetime—likened so often to the brief flowering of the cherries—in such a way that he will have no regrets. And the decision he makes, we may say, will determine the entire shape of his life.

When the ordinary person gives some thought to his life and how it should be lived, he finds himself confronted by an impenetrable barrier, a basic problem that, no matter how many times he may turn it over in his mind, he cannot solve. As a result, he usually finds, he has little choice but to abandon the effort.

This basic problem, needless to say, is the problem of human life and death. At least so far as we can tell at present, there seems to be no mechanism by which a man can will his own birth. We may therefore, I assume, agree in a sense with the existentialist philosophers who see man as a lonely being cast into the world for no reason at all.

This life which man has been involuntarily plunged into, however, is in one sense nothing more than an inexorable progress toward death, the negation of life. From the instant of his birth, man begins moving toward this final destination. Moreover, though man is conscious of the fact that death awaits him, and though there exist means such as suicide by which he may voluntarily end his life, in most cases society does not permit him the freedom to resort to them. Thus we may say that birth and death are both irrevocably determined in a dimension far removed from the free will of the individual. Man merely drifts along in the stream of birth and death.

Many persons, confronting the conditions governing human life, see them as almost unbearably severe, and are filled with despair and a distaste for life. There are also those who, convinced that no amount of thinking will remedy the matter, end up as hedonists, determined to derive as much enjoyment as they can from the brief time allotted them.

I do not intend here to discuss which attitude is preferable, nor do I feel I have the right to insist that people adopt one approach rather than another. I merely wish to state my view that, although we are all of us as human beings subject to these same conditions, we will never be able to grasp the full meaning and truth of human life unless we stop at some point to examine the nature of our existence.

Someone has stated that a person is ready for a revolution in his life the moment he realizes he is being conditioned and manipulated by outside forces beyond his comprehension. In most cases, of course, the strongest and most direct motivation for such a revolution has its origin in the dissatisfactions and frustrations of daily life. Yet at the same time the irritating sense of being bound by forces outside oneself, when one really ought to be the author of one's own destiny, surely constitutes a basic impetus for undertaking a human revolution.

Karl Marx claimed to discover in the mechanism of society the forces which bind and manipulate men. But if we look no further than this, we can never hope to solve the more fundamental question of why man is condemned by external forces to undergo a meaningless progression of birth and death.

This being the case, we must direct the tools of analysis to this question of the bonds of life and death itself. Only when we can evolve some philosophy that will provide a solution to this question, I believe, can men be freed from their most deep-seated fears. And when human beings, using the radical viewpoint of such a philosophy as their point of departure, come to reconstitute themselves, they will find themselves facing a new and bright dawn. Then even the problems of alienation can be solved. I cannot help feeling that this is a task which the condition of contemporary civilization forces upon us.

SELF-REALIZATION

Now that I know
the emptiness of the world,
deeper and deeper,
greater and greater grows my sorrow.
Ōtomo no Tabito (665–731)

While Tabito was serving as Governor-General of the Dazaifu in Kyushu, his wife Ōtomo no Iratsume died. The poem above was written in response to letters of condolence received from friends in the capital. For a person who has actually experienced such a loss, the poem will undoubtedly be even more moving than for the ordinary reader. The well-known critic Mokichi Saitō points out that it is one of the earliest lyric poems to deal in a philosophical manner with the uncertainty of life, and believes that it must have possessed considerable novelty and freshness at the time of its composition.

Buddhism—as soon as people in Japan hear the word, they tend to think of such concepts as the evanescence of life or of *yūgen*, the kind of mysterious beauty that is the ideal of the Nō drama and medieval poetry. Such associations, I cannot help feeling, arise because people view Buddhism too much in aesthetic terms. True Buddhism is concerned with a very practical problem—how man should live his life—and never for an instant allows its attention to be diverted from that problem. And because this is its purpose, it demands as a first step that one conduct a thorough and fearless examination into the true nature of human life.

As an example, we may note the motivations which led Shakyamuni, the founder of Buddhism, to take up the religious life. Legend describes these as the Outings from the Four Gates. When Shakyamuni, the son of the ruler of the state, was living in the royal palace, he decided he would take a pleasure trip outside the walls of the city. When he emerged from the east gate, however, he saw an old man. Another time, going out from the south gate, he saw a sick man, and going out from the west gate, he saw a dead man. Finally, when he went out from the north gate, he saw a man who had taken up the religious life and, deeply moved, he decided to leave his family and follow the same kind of life himself.

This is an anecdote of great interest and importance, it seems to me, for although it may be no more than legend, it sums up in symbolic form the point of departure of Buddhism. It makes clear that the fundamental aim of Buddhism is to examine the basic ills of human existence and to discover some way to conquer them. These fundamental ills are described in Buddhism as the Four Sufferings, the miseries inflicted on man by birth, old age, sickness, and death.

We speak of human life, or of man's good fortune or bad fortune, but in the end these refer simply to the succession of ups and downs experienced from moment to moment by the life force within man and the sensations of pleasure or grief which they produce. The question of how this life force can be most effectively directed, therefore, is one of fundamental importance to the existence of mankind, one whose importance transcends all considerations of time.

Shakyamuni eventually gained enlightenment and perceived the Truth that would solve the problem of human suffering. But as he looked about him at the mass of men, he saw that they were engulfed in misery and showed no inclination to turn their thoughts to the basic problem of human life. Moreover, currents of hedonism were strong in the society of his time, sweeping men along in a frantic and never-ending search for immediate gratification of the senses. Under such circumstances, it is not surprising that the men of the time, engrossed in the struggles of daily life, felt disinclined to bother their heads about the eternal problems of existence.

Nowadays one seldom hears the technical Buddhist term *rokudō rinne*, which means, "transmigration through the Six Paths," that is, the six states or worlds of existence. If we ignore the air of pedantry that attaches to such a term and try to understand what it originally referred to, I think we might paraphrase it in modern language by saying it means being buried in the trivia of everyday existence. That is, men who are in one of these six states of existence are, like the masses in Shakyamuni's time, completely engrossed in their daily lives.

No one would deny that there is a certain universality to human nature that transcends the passage of time. On that basis, I would like to venture a leap of the imagination. Put into plain words, I believe what Shakyamuni was saying to people was simply this: *Just for once, you must somehow break away from everyday existence. And when you do, then for the first time your eyes will be opened to the meaning of human life!* Furthermore, it seems to me that the emphasis he placed on the ephemeral and ever-changing nature of life represents merely a preliminary step toward the objective of learning how to establish the permanent self in the midst of that ephemerality.

I have spoken of the six states of existence in which one is immersed in the concerns of the everyday world. But Buddhism recognizes other states of existence, among them *engaku* or *dokkaku*, the one of self-enlightenment. This is the state of a person who, by observing the passing of the seasons and meditating upon the concepts of suffering, the emptiness of the phenomenal world, impermanence, and the nonexistence of the ego, attains enlightenment through his own efforts. If I were to describe the state in modern terms, I would say that it is that of the person who seeks to gain enlightenment through philosophical or artistic means.

Another state of existence is that known as *shōmon*, that of the person who achieves enlightenment by listening to the preaching of a Buddha. It might be described as that of the person who seeks the truth through doctrine and intellectual inquiry. Both of these states of existence represent pinnacles of achievement reached by reflective individuals who have succeeded in breaking away completely from the realm of everyday life. These individuals have created for themselves their own inner world. And when a person is dwelling in one of these narrow self-made worlds, his main concern invariably becomes the question of inner spiritual refinement and perfection.

At this point arises the concept of *keshin metchi* or "the annihilation of the body and the destruction of consciousness." The person who is attempting to maintain his hold upon the perfect inner world of his construction finds that his own self, beset as it is with numberless worries and delusions, becomes the greatest obstacle to success. He therefore determines to do away with the self, and what is known figuratively as "the annihilation of the body and the destruction of consciousness" becomes his ideal.

This is a classic example of a journey having as its starting point the pursuit of life and leading eventually to a kind of death. It might in fact be called the aesthetics of death. Paradoxically it could just as well be described as a hymn of praise to life, for its goal represents a distant world attainable only by soaring far above the trivia of daily existence. In "Thoughts on Life and Death" I mention the extraordinary beauty which the novelist Akutagawa was able to perceive just before his death. It was a beauty perceived through the light of an interior world of the kind we have been discussing.

The establishment of this inner world is, first and last, sought for the sake of life. When a person realizes the extent to which he is trapped and buried in the exterior realms of everyday existence, it is natural for him to extricate himself. But once he has done so, he must eventually return again to the everyday world of reality. When we speak of living a better life, we mean, do we not, this process of endless coming and going between these interior and exterior worlds of existence.

The *shōmon* and *engaku* states of existence certainly represent very lofty and admirable levels of enlightenment. However, they are achieved, strictly speaking, by rejecting the everyday world of reality, removing oneself from human activities—what Akutagawa called "the trivia of life"—and seeking complete immersion in an inner world. The reason persons of a certain type are so often depicted as living in quiet seclusion far removed from human habitation and devoting themselves to contemplation and meditation is undoubtedly because they are searching for this kind of self-realization.

In the Mahayana scriptures, persons who have reached the level of the *shōmon* and *engaku* and then remain there are roundly condemned. This is because, having advanced to the very threshold of the true meaning of life, they cease their efforts and rest where they are, content to settle for an inferior type of enlightenment. In fact, however, the question of how to live one's life and achieve self-realization can only be solved by applying oneself to the task of saving others from the miseries that beset them. This is the way of the *bosatsu* or bodhisattva, the state of existence above the *shōmon* and *engaku*. To follow such a way means to strive for the salvation of the masses at the same time that one strives for inner self-realization.

To seek to discover how the interior and exterior worlds of man interact and stimulate one another is, needless to say, one of the ultimate tasks of scholarship and art as well as of religion. But both art and scholarship possess their own autonomous realms. One may therefore be led to approve only the type of self-realization to be found within his particular realm. In my view, however, self-realization in the true meaning of the word is something achieved only through communication with the everyday world of external reality.

The breezes blowing over me from the garden are delightful. On such a clear, refreshing morning, why have I become engrossed in these rambling thoughts? Could it be because I have just learned of the suicide of the novelist Yasunari Kawabata?

THE JAPANESE SPIRIT

The other day I went to a flower arrangement show held by a friend of mine. The exhibitors were nonprofessionals, housewives or people working in offices who were busy most of the time with other things. Still, they had found the time to participate in this show, which represented no particular school of flower arrangement but simply the creative and cooperative efforts of everyone involved.

The arrangements were grouped into four sections representing the concepts of earth, water, fire, and wind. A professional teacher of flower arrangement viewing the results would probably find them far from perfect, nothing more than expressions of the naive artistic sense of the ordinary run of people. And yet there was an air of youthful vitality about these two hundred and fifty or more arrangements. To me, it made them a richly poetic embodiment of the Japanese spirit.

I was delighted and deeply impressed. The men and women of traditional Japan, with their highly refined sensibility, learned to respond to the plants and flowers of nature and to create through them a beauty of the highest order. And I could see that that spirit was still very much alive among the ordinary people even today, when the natural environment is being destroyed with alarming rapidity. I also realized that in present-day Japan in particular, where people are obliged to plod through dull and tiresome daily routines like so many draft horses, it is imperative to have a modicum of leisure, to relax and enjoy such things as flower arrangement and the tea ceremony.

Engrossed in thoughts such as these and thoroughly enjoying myself, I suddenly discovered that I had spent over an hour among them.

Come to think of it, I suppose Japan is the only country where the arranging of flowers has been raised to the level of a fine art, and the same probably applies to the tea ceremony. This leads me to wonder if the Japanese as a people haven't always been oriented toward sensitivity and emotionally based concepts. I certainly know nothing about the inner mysteries of the various schools of flower arrangement and the tea ceremony, but I do know that the spirit underlying these pursuits would be very difficult to describe and evaluate in terms of Western concepts of reason and intellect.

The same type of sensitivity is found in that most typical of Japanese verse forms, the haiku, particularly in the fact that the haiku invariably includes some indication of the season in which the poem is set. Though one of the briefest and most compressed of all verse forms, the haiku demands the inclusion of a word indicative of the season so that the reader may properly grasp the mood and feeling of the poem. Similarly, the Japanese have over the centuries developed a number of distinctive aesthetic ideals such as *wabi*, a tone of quiet and restraint; *sabi*, a tone of loneliness and faded beauty; or *fūryū*, elegance and refinement. These concepts, it seems to me, are not derived from any logical process or cognition; rather they were fostered by persons of highly acute sensibility who were attempting thereby to give expression to the subtle moods and changes of nature.

There was a time here and abroad when it was very popular to indulge in theories about the Japanese personality. As one of its defects, it was pointed out that no people are so given to vagueness in their modes of expression. Even our way of smiling was singled out for its vagueness and ambiguity and, with more than a trace of contempt, was dubbed "the Japanese smile." At international conferences and gatherings it has become a common occurrence for Japanese speakers to take the podium and deliver greetings so imprecise and understated as to be the despair of the interpreters. Among Japanese, however, such fuzzy amenities are understood perfectly well. No hostess in the West, I am told, would be likely to urge her guests to help themselves to the food set before them by saying, "Actually, there's nothing at all to eat . . ." This is the custom in Japan. On the other hand, if a Japanese hostess were to follow Western custom and announce to her guests, "Have some of this because it's very good!" they would be distinctly on their guard.

The peculiarly Japanese phrases used in social situations all have a good reason for existing, it seems to me, though admittedly they may sound strange to others. Even the custom of stating things in a vague manner is to some extent a deliberate device to avoid hurting the feelings of the other party or spoiling the human relationship by seeming to take too legalistic an approach. It is, you might say, characteristic Japanese wisdom to try to establish a relationship of mutual trust and understanding with others, rather than to insist upon spelling everything out in a clear and logical fashion.

These contrasting approaches to human relationships are emphasized in Ruth Benedict's *The Chrysanthemum and the Sword*, a widely read work on the Japanese character by a Western anthropologist. I remember reading the book and feeling abashed and to some degree resentful at the penetrating way in which she singled out the characteristics of the Japanese people and the particular patterns of our culture. Perhaps because I was still quite young, I had, I recall, a rather complicated reaction to the book. I tried hard not to be taken in by the cool logic of her arguments, and yet in the end I would find myself compelled to accept them.

Benedict, as is well known, compares Japanese culture with that of the West and, in apt phrases that have since become famous, characterizes the former as a "shame culture" and the latter as a "guilt culture." In other words, the ethical concept exercising the greatest influence in Japanese society is, according to her analysis, that of shame. Whether for good or for bad, it is this concept, the consciousness of shame, the feeling that one cannot hold up one's head before others if one does or does not do certain things, which serves as the basis for Japanese patterns of behavior.

In contrast to this stands the concept of guilt as it functions in the West. If one has done something bad, or one is, for example, a mother whose son has committed some misdeed, then one will be bothered first of all by one's conscience and by personal feelings of guilt, and will be only secondarily concerned about what society or the world as a whole thinks of one. In this sense, it has been traditional in the West to base individual judgments of good and evil upon the dictates of inner conscience. The Japanese, by contrast, have been rather weak in a sense of personal inner conscience, tending rather to be guided by their sense of responsibility toward society and their wish to avoid incurring shame in its eyes.

What Professor Benedict wished to demonstrate by this analysis of the Japanese psyche was that the Japanese do not develop a strict sense of rationalism and truth based upon acutely reasoned personal judgments. This, she went on to emphasize, was one of the reasons why Japan lagged behind in modernization.

Ever since her book came out, I have the feeling that these categories of "shame culture" and "guilt culture" have, explicitly or implicitly, formed the basis for every discussion and analysis of the Japanese character. In the period following the end of the Pacific War, when democracy was in the process of being established, many Japanese intellectuals borrowed Benedict's theories and modified them in various ways, using them in their efforts to enlighten their countrymen, to establish Western style concepts of the ego, and to promote a spirit of rationalism.

There are many points made in *The Chrysanthemum and the Sword* that as a Japanese I feel one should pay heed to. As I think back dispassionately over the ideas of the book, however, it does not seem to me that there is anything in it that would call for an all-out rejection or denial of Japanese ways of thinking.

Certainly as individuals we must all strive to develop inner standards and habits of sound reasoning. Nevertheless, in the course of human life one will find that he cannot deal with all situations merely on the basis of the theoretical categories produced by reasoning and discrimination. And if one tries forcibly to do so, he is likely to become the kind of person who is a slave to his own logic and theory. In the West such subservience to an absolute ideal has often prevailed. And when it does so, whether the absolute be a deity, an ideology, or a concept such as science, it is allowed to take precedence over man himself and leads to bitter experiences that in the end estrange man from it.

Certainly we must allow no compromise when it comes to distinctions between true and false or judgments of good and evil. To permit such distinctions to become blurred by ambiguity would be decidedly wrong. But when one is living one's life as an ordinary individual in the present-day world, then I cannot help feeling that a certain amount of gentle vagueness, a sense of shame deriving from a humble appraisal of one's

107

own character, add a special flavor to living, a spice to the human experience. We would be poorer without it.

The simple beauty of the cherry blossoms, so pale in hue—one can hardly tell if they are colored at all—and the sensitive Japanese spirit that knows how to perceive the beauty in such flowers—these seem to come together in my thoughts on this spring day.

YESTERDAY, TODAY

This spring I had a chance to visit Europe, my first trip there in some time. I spent about ten days in Paris and a week in London, and then had to go on to the United States. It was a hurried trip but from it I feel I gained a great deal.

Whether in Paris, London, or some other European city, I am always impressed with the way the things of the past are prized. History continues to live in the present. Walking through the streets of Paris, one notices a number of buildings with the date they were erected inscribed on them. Structures a hundred or even a hundred and fifty years old are not in the least rare. And among the more imposing buildings, those with a history attached to them, are some that date back two or three hundred years.

What I admire about these structures is the way they continue even now to function as vital areas for the citizens of Paris. On the ground floor facing the street are pleasant shops, while the upper floors are given over to apartments. Even on main thoroughfares in the busiest part of the city it is rare to find buildings reserved wholly for business. There is no sharp line separating the places where people live and the places where they conduct their business. This, it seems to me, is what accounts for the dynamic character of the streets of Paris.

In Japan, too, in such places as Nara and Kyoto, there are buildings dating far back into the past. Most, however, are structures of a special nature, such as temples, and they therefore do not function as places where people conduct their daily activities. Indeed, these buildings often no longer fill even their original roles as temples but are preserved simply as cultural monuments, something for tourists to visit and admire. This means that as buildings they have ceased to be functional, have ceased to be alive.

There are of course a number of old buildings within the city of London, but I was particularly impressed with the ones we saw on our visits to Oxford and Cambridge. On the way to Oxford we stopped to rest in what appeared to be a farmhouse, built in the fourteenth century, I was told. The simple lines of the blackened beams and posts and the extremely solid way in which they were fitted together gave one an indescribable feeling of tranquility and repose.

Oxford and Cambridge boast colleges founded in the twelfth and thirteenth centuries. Even now these tradition-filled seats of learning are training young people for the twenty-first century. On being shown some of the student rooms, I learned that even the furniture has remained unchanged from centuries past. Students, it seems, feel proud to study in the same room and at the same desk as some famous alumnus who made a name for himself in history.

Taking care of old things—no, more than that, actually continuing to put them to use—cannot be explained as mere frugality or miserliness. The furniture or the old buildings I saw, the town itself or even the natural surroundings are all material things and presumably can be assigned a certain economic value. But when such material things have become intimately involved in human activities, when history has become etched on them, they are no longer simply pieces of matter. They become objects which cannot be described merely in terms of economic value.

What inspires this desire of the French and the English to continue to use the things of the past and to treat them with respect? Is it not a deep-seated determination to prevent the history of the past from melting away? It would seem that this attitude is infused with a feeling of reverence toward the activities of the men of the past, activities which have in some way become an integral part of these historical objects. Needless to say, this attitude acts as a powerful restraining force in determining the way men in present-day England and France conduct their lives.

There is a sense in which history has perhaps come to be regarded with excessive reverence in modern day England, which may result in a certain undue constriction of behavior. If so, then it is not appropriate simply to say that the more reverence paid to history, the better. Some balance must be struck between the preservation of the past and progress.

As far as the Japanese of today are concerned, it would be difficult to overemphasize this need for balance, though for quite the opposite reason. In Japan, priceless legacies of the past are one after another being wiped out, destroyed without the slightest consideration for the rich cultural and historical values they embody. The destruction is not limited merely to our man-made cultural heritage. We go a step further, heartlessly ravaging the forests, lakes, and seas, parts of our natural heritage which have been millions of years in the making.

Apparently even we Japanese once had the custom of regarding old things with a sense of reverence and preserving them with care. Our forefathers believed that the spirits of their ancestors resided in the cultural objects that they had made and used, spirits that would be deeply angered if the objects were not treated with respect. In the lakes and forests they believed there were nature deities dwelling, who would put a curse on anyone attempting to despoil their domains. Looking at it from the vantage point of the present, one can appreciate the shrewd wisdom of our forebears in fostering such ideas.

In more recent times, however, such beliefs in the power of angry spirits or the curse of the gods have come to be regarded as mere superstitions conjured up by our fear-ridden ancestors. By now we have arrived at the point where, for the sake of immediate profit, we lay waste to nature without the slightest fear or hesitation. Thus virgin forests are felled to make way for more profitable stands of cryptomeria and cypress, and lakes are utilized for the disposal of wastes until they become foul with industrial pollution.

The result? The legendary curses predicted by our ancestors seem to be on the point of materializing, and in forms more terrible than they could have anticipated. The contamination of the lakes and rivers and seas has begun to afflict those who live near them with strange new maladies, and the cutting down of the forests has brought on floods and landslides.

Moreover, as we destroy the cultural treasures inherited from ancient times, we further expand the desert of alienation and mutual mistrust that afflicts our society. There is a serious danger in this. Our present propensity to evaluate everything in materialistic and economic terms and to ignore spiritual and humanistic considerations will be passed on to future generations, inflicting the same errors of judgment upon them and condemning them to suffer even graver consequences.

Our forefathers handed down to us an attitude of awe toward the gods and the spirits of the dead. In contemporary terms we might describe it as a respect for the spiritual, for the human aspects underlying material things. Or perhaps we can think of it as the will to be in harmony with the forces and rhythms of the natural world. We have become aware of the importance of this attitude, however, only after having been cursed severely as a result of our neglect of it. If we can somehow learn to cherish these ancient concepts of the spirits and gods and humbly consider their true meaning, then this attitude of the ancients may once more become a vital part of the thinking of contemporary man.

After the middle of the previous century the Japanese adopted elements of European science and technology and succeeded in building a modern technological society. But they took from the West only the end products, the techniques and material aspects of European civilization, and ignored, it would seem, the morality and humanistic attitudes, the prime movers of that culture. Too anxious to pursue and overtake the West, the Japanese purchased a superb engine but neglected to find out how to apply the brakes.

The brakes, in effect, are something that must come from the individual himself, something that must arise out of an inner spiritual change. In this sense, we may say that Japan still has a great deal to learn from Europe.

THOUGHTS
ON LIFE AND DEATH

The film *To Die for Love* (*Mourir d'aimer*) is extremely popular in Japan. Or at least that's what I hear from my younger friends. Unfortunately I rarely get to the movies these days.

Set against the 1968 May Revolution in France, this movie is said to be based on an actual love affair between a thirty-two-year-old teacher and one of her seventeen-year-old male students. For a time the lovers in their passionate sincerity succeed in resisting the numerous pressures brought to bear on them, but eventually charges are filed against the teacher in court. Deeply wounded in spirit, she commits suicide.

We associate France with Paris and Paris with love and gaiety. The truth is, France has a dark side too, the old and extremely rigid social order depicted in *To Die for Love*. Apparently the movie was filmed with the purpose of registering a strong protest against that order.

One plausible reason for the film's popularity among youth in Japan is the profound impression made by the readiness of the hero and heroine to risk everything for the sake of love. At first glance, the young adults of today seem indifferent to such things, scoffing at sentimentality and declaring that risking one's life for any cause at all is mere "nonsense." And yet, deep down, the hearts of Japanese youth have clearly been touched, even by the rather quaint and old-fashioned notion of sacrificing one's life for the sake of love.

What does it mean to love someone? Miss Ayako Sono, author of a current best-selling novel, defines it as a willingness "to die for the one you love." True love, and the tragedies which it often entails, have of course been frequent themes in literature from ages past. *The Love Sui-*

113

cides of Amijima and other works of the seventeenth century Japanese playwright Chikamatsu that deal with the subject of love-suicide are outstanding examples. In these works, the unfortunate lovers, caught in a web of social duties and obligations, find that fulfilling their love can be accomplished only by the act of choosing death.

What moves us about these dramas is the fact that the more the lovers are bound and frustrated by social conventions, the more intense their passion becomes, until it culminates in the final outpouring of devotion and they are able to transcend the fear of death. For us today, who live in a sterile and mechanized society where so much emphasis is placed upon mere sexual gratification, something in the plays awakens in us a secret feeling of envy and admiration, admiration for the lovers whose passion is so great that it makes them willing to sacrifice their lives.

To be willing to risk death in order to live the kind of life one believes in—this is the key to understanding and realizing to the fullest what it really means to be alive.

I was deeply impressed when I heard a famous Japanese author tell how he happened to become a writer. Growing into manhood during the Pacific War, he had fully resigned himself to going off to the front. He was never in terror of dying. But each time the thought of it flashed through his mind, he became more intensely aware of how irreplaceable were the moments of life remaining to him. The memory of these youthful experiences and the desire to understand the true meaning and awe of life, he reported, were what led him to take up the pursuit of literature.

Before 1945 many young men in Japan believed that life was something one should be prepared to sacrifice for the sake of one's country. And in fact many of them did, tragically ending their youthful lives on the field of battle.

After 1945, however, an intense reaction against such thinking set in, and it came to be regarded as anachronistic to believe that there was anything at all worth risking one's life for. Even today the young people who have no memory of the war seem to be groping restlessly for something to give meaning to life in the midst of the emptiness of daily existence. The uneasy feelings of the young manifest themselves in various ways, driving some to reject the entire Establishment and its values and adopt the life style of the hippies. In the case of others, the uneasiness erupts in the form of violent resistance to the established order.

A newspaper article I read recently about prison inmates brought home to me how an awareness of death can affect one's whole attitude toward life. According to the article, men on death row show an acute sensitivity to their surroundings and are given to almost abnormally intense moods of alternating delight and anger, elation and melancholy. By contrast, the emotional responses of the lifers, it was found, become increasingly feeble until, indifferent to their surroundings, they lose their entire individuality in a generalized posture of servile obedience.

The writer of the article concluded by comparing the psychological malaise of the lifers with the malaise of those "sentenced to life" in our present "managed" society. Certainly all of us must at one time or another feel that whatever freedom we have in modern society is so circumscribed and "managed" by forces beyond our control that we can no longer make any truly vital response to life.

Now and again some individual decides, however, that he can no longer allow his life to be prescribed. On November 25, 1970, we were shocked to learn about the grim suicide of Yukio Mishima, the internationally acclaimed novelist and playwright. Here was a man who had refused to be managed, who had chosen to die for his principles. When the mass media showed Mishima as he pled, several minutes before his death, with the members of the Japanese Self-Defense Forces, charging them to act like true soldiers instead of salaried employees, I suppose many of us realized that, though his demands may have sounded irrational, Mishima's pleas constituted a challenge to an age incapable of honestly facing up to either life or death.

Surely anyone who faces imminent death becomes intensely aware of life, since so few moments of it remain to him. An apt example is the experience of the famous novelist Ryunosuke Akutagawa. Before he committed suicide in 1927 at the age of thirty-five, he commented how remarkably beautiful all of nature seemed to him. And it seemed so, he reflected, because he viewed it through eyes that were about to close forever.

Personally, however, I feel somewhat unhappy about the implication that it is only through the thought of death that one can become aware of the meaning of life. Must a man face imminent demise before he can understand what it means to be alive? This seems to me too shallow and limiting an outlook, because it persists in viewing life and death as separate and opposing entities.

Not long ago I was struck by an observation regarding widely divergent ways of looking at life and death. In the course of conversations with Count R. E. Coudenhove-Kalergi, a proponent of European unity, we touched on this question. The Count pointed out that people in the East tend to think of life and death as a single page in a book, a page which, when it comes to an end, can be turned so that one may move on to another page. By contrast, people in the West tend to think of birth, or the beginning of life, as the first page, and death as the last page of a book. This simile, it seems to me, trenchantly illustrates these two contrasting ways of looking at life and death.

Life as an endlessly continuing succession of births and deaths. This is the Asian view. And in this view, one must seek his goal and mission in something that transcends birth and death, something that he is willing to risk his life for. Only then can he arrive at a true realization of the inexhaustible nature of life. In other words, he must advance beyond the mere struggle to stay alive and be prepared to ask himself for what purpose he lives his life.

Each person must try to discover the particular theme or motif that he believes should characterize his life. An attitude of intense seriousness toward each fleeting moment of life, which at the same time knows no feeling of regret regardless of when death may come, can change one's whole way of living.

We saw examples of such commitment in this morning's paper, which reported how thousands of young Japanese turned out to demonstrate in support of International Anti-War Day. Once again youthful energies were expended, youthful hopes were frustrated and dashed against the pavement. These young men and women on the streets of Tokyo in 1971 somehow merged in my mind's eye with pictures I had seen of French youths carrying anti-Establishment banners on the streets of Paris in 1968. The faces of those who fell wounded during these demonstrations continue to haunt me.

116

STRONGHOLDS FOR PEACE

Recently I read *The Battle of Okinawa*, one volume in a series of works in Japanese put out by the Ryukyuan government on the history of Okinawa Prefecture. It deals with the American bombardment and invasion of the island in 1945, a battle that claimed the lives of over 200 thousand persons.

It is a shocking document made up of interviews with a thousand anonymous persons who describe the horrors they experienced. Its lengthy pages contain very little in the way of overt antiwar sentiment or ideological protest. The narrative does not venture beyond a plain recording of the facts, surprising rather for the restrained and unimpassioned manner in which they are presented. The very simplicity and starkness of the narrative grip the reader and stir him to the depths of his being. Again and again as I read along I found myself overcome with anger and indignation.

One of the most painful passages relates the experiences of a farm wife of Aragusuku, who was thirty-nine at the time. When the U.S. naval bombardment began, she and the other members of her family fled for shelter to a nearby ditch, but as the fighting advanced they were driven from place to place in a frantic and endless search for safety. In the course of their flight, one after another of the members of the woman's family were struck down.

The first victim was her eighteen-year-old daughter, who, in attempting to nurse the injured, was hit in the back by shrapnel as she was washing her face in a stream. She died three days later. The woman's younger sister was also wounded in the back, and died two hours later.

117

"Everything was in such confusion I couldn't stop to look after each one of them. My five-year-old daughter was wounded in the wrist and the stomach and her insides were coming out. She was already dead by that time, but my mother was making such a commotion that I became confused and began screaming, 'Grandma is stomping on my little girl and making her insides come out!' All the time my mother was insisting she wasn't doing any such thing."

With the shelling still going on around her, the woman continued to flee in search of shelter. "We had taken refuge in an empty house in Shin'eipei. I guess the bombardment must have started again, because this time I was hit by a piece of shell. I had my year-and-a-half-old baby in my arms; his wrist and right arm and forehead and chest were all cut and bleeding. My second son Tsutomu had a gash in his head and was knocked flat by the impact of the explosion. When I looked around, I discovered that my mother-in-law had been killed outright in the explosion. . . .

"My aunt was killed at Shingaki. The shells and the explosions there were terrible. Pieces of human flesh came flying through the air out of nowhere. The bodies were piled up all over."

The woman's little baby died shortly after from lack of food. All told, the woman lost ten members of her immediate family as a result of the fighting. What a fearful slaughter!

And yet her experiences were by no means exceptional. Nearly every one of the thousand persons interviewed has much the same sort of story to tell. In fact there are probably persons besides those interviewed who could relate even more ghastly stories of the fate inflicted upon them. One woman, asked by those who were gathering material if she would describe her experiences, refused to say anything beyond, "If you get me started talking about the war, I'm afraid I might go right out of my mind and end up by attacking you!"

What cruel and pitiful scars war leaves! How stupid and senseless is its destruction! And always it is the nameless masses of people who are condemned to suffer and groan and weep in the midst of the gore and flames. It is their cries, the cries of men and women who have no one to appeal to, that we must harken to and respect, for their voices ring with a truth and sincerity far more compelling than any lofty statement of pacifist principles. Their cries must serve as the point of departure for any meaningful movement to oppose warfare and bring about lasting peace.

Unfortunately, men continue to overlook this fact, perhaps because they consider the cries of these anonymous human beings too common-place to serve as a point of departure. And for this very reason the horrors of the Okinawan experience continue to be reenacted in areas throughout the world, their stench still with us today.

Auschwitz, Hiroshima, Nagasaki, the Korean War, the war in Vietnam, East Pakistan—looking only at the conflicts and tragedies of the past twenty or thirty years is enough to persuade us that history is a never-ending succession of human crimes and follies.

In *Harken to the Voice of the Deep!*, a collection of notes written by young Japanese students who later died in the Pacific War, there is a passage which speaks out scathingly against such folly: "Bestiality—how deeply it is rooted in the nature of man! At heart, I cannot help feeling that ever since man created this world of his, he has not made the slightest degree of progress. The present war is not a matter of right or justice, whatever others may say. It is nothing but an eruption of hatred among peoples, and the fighting will no doubt continue until both sides have wiped each other out. How fearful, how despicable! Mankind, truly a cousin of the apes!"

And yet the kind of sincere humanism which might combat such folly and engender a true sense of love and justice among mankind seems to be powerless to make itself heard in the realm of international politics. Despite the cries of outrage and opposition raised throughout the world, nation after nation continues to carry out nuclear tests.

Why is the bestiality of man allowed free rein? Simply, I would submit, because the doctrine of nationalism and national interest encourages and lends justification to man's baser instincts. To combat these tendencies, it is necessary for each of us as individuals, no matter how weak or inef-fectual we may feel ourselves to be, to build deep within our hearts a stronghold for peace, one that will be capable of withstanding and in the end silencing the incessant calls to war. This is the only way man's tragic predilections for violence can be reformed and his energies chan-neled into new directions.

119

Some may scoff at the naiveté and sentimentalism of such an appeal, claiming that it takes no cognizance of the complex political realities of our time. But if it is sentimentalism to try to do what has to be done in the only way in which it can be done, then I am content to suffer the charge. Right now, the most important question, I believe, is how we can utilize the sense of pain and outrage that one experiences in reading a work such as *The Battle of Okinawa* and effectively expand it until it grows into a universal outcry for peace.

The term "nuclear allergy" has often been used in Japan in recent years, meaning, I assume, that the Japanese are overly sensitive in matters pertaining to nuclear armament. But if we cease to be sensitive to the prospect of war, if we develop an immunity and callousness even to the horrors of nuclear weaponry, then from that instant on we will indeed be in danger of destruction. And with each repeated testing of nuclear weapons, the dark shadow of that moment seems to draw closer.

I have visited Okinawa many times. With its deep blue sky so characteristic of tropical regions, its coral seas, its dazzling sunlight, it is a place of superb natural beauty and freshness. And yet, by contrast, how gloomy and oppressive is the atmosphere of the human world existing amidst the beauty of nature. It is a society that lives in the shadow of armaments and military installations, strategies and maneuverings for world power and domination. The monster of war, which once in the past turned this beautiful island into a living hell, seems still to brood ominously over it. More ominously, I'm afraid, now than ever before.

ANALYSIS
AND SYNTHESIS

The garden in winter,
strings of moonlight to go with
the insect's song.

Bashō

It is the time of the year when the moon and stars shine clear and beautiful in the chilly night sky, already winter by the calendar of Bashō's time. Off to the south Orion, the ruler of midwinter nights, is looming into view, two stars of the first magnitude and two stars of the second magnitude poised in a great rectangle, in their midst a string of three stars slanting boldly downward. The "Three Great Stars" they were called by the Japanese in past times, who were as familiar with the constellation as the stargazers of the West.

Sei Shōnagon, the famous woman writer of eleventh century Japan, on the other hand, declares in her *Pillow Book* that "among stars, the Pleiades are the best!" They too, part of the constellation Taurus, are in sight now, twinkling away mysteriously.

Nowadays, however, these eternal beauties of the natural world more often than not are hidden from view behind a thick smog spreading like a curtain across the sky, a product of our cities' heavy industries, and the beams of light, greetings sent to us from points thousands and even millions of light-years away, are heartlessly intercepted. It is a situation we all regret. And yet, perhaps because we see them less often, on the rare occasions when the smog lifts, the shining of these faraway heavenly bodies seems to remind us more poignantly than ever of how petty are the daily frets and worries of our human world.

Man and the stars—it is a theme to inspire endless tales and fantasies. One thinks in particular of how man in ancient times, gazing up at the shining constellations, saw in them the heroes of his mythology. They made him aware of his own existence as a dweller within the vast folds of the universe, and he tried to use them as a means to lift himself above the endless vicissitudes of daily life.

Among these countless stars and planets, one has suddenly become a focus of interest. Mars, glowing with a red light almost ominous in its intensity, has within the past few months approached closer to the earth than at any time in the last fifteen years. In order to take advantage of this unparalleled opportunity, a tiny man-made "star" has been sent spinning off on a lengthy journey into space, and even now is circling the Red Planet, attempting to get a glimpse of its face. As I look up into the night sky, I know it is impossible to see the little satellite; yet I am sure it is there, hovering over the surface of Mars and snapping pictures.

Someone commented that launching a satellite into space and placing it in orbit around a planet millions of miles away is rather like standing some thirty feet away from a vending machine and trying to toss a coin into its slot. That modern science, through its vast accumulation of knowledge and the incredible accuracy of its analytical powers, has been able to accomplish this seemingly impossible feat is a fact we must all stand in awe of.

There is a note of irony too. Although the computers which have made such accomplishments possible are capable of setting a rocket on its course with the most precise degree of accuracy, they cannot predict where a sheet of paper will land when dropped from a distance of no more than three feet or so from the ground. As one computer expert explained to me, it is a widespread but wholly mistaken assumption to believe that computers can come up with answers to any problem posed to them. They can supply answers, of course, only to those problems they have been programmed to deal with. "Predicting when an earthquake or a landslide will occur or what course a typhoon will follow—problems such as these they are incapable of handling, much less matters concerned with the inner workings of the human mind," he confessed to me with a candor that I knew must have come from the heart.

Modern man with his scientific knowledge has succeeded in inventing pesticides to control damage to crops and chemical fertilizers to increase agricultural productivity. But that same wisdom and knowledge failed to warn him to what extent he would thereby upset the delicate balance of nature or what effects these products might eventually have on the environment in which he lives.

Though the glory of modern science, like a highly polished blade, sheds its light on all areas of life, when we examine the achievements of science as a whole, we see that there is something distorted in that light, something far removed from the artless and uncontrived beauty of the lights shining in the world of nature.

In the area of analysis, science has indisputably made dramatic progress. In that other most important area of synthesis—not the breaking down of data but the building up of comprehensive theories and principles— what has it contributed? Needless to say, the problems of synthesis are not ones to be solved by science alone. So long as we continue simply to ignore them, we can never hope for smooth and harmonious development in human society.

I recall a penetrating remark made by one scholar which may be pertinent at this point. "Viewed in the light of the traditional spirit of science, the results achieved in such fields as microbiology may represent enormous progress," he observed. "But from the human standpoint, from the point of view of a living individual, who knows he is faced with inevitable death, I wonder if they really deserve to be called progress at all."

Microbiology is said to be one of the most advanced fields of modern science. It is a discipline that seeks to analyze the living organism down to the very atoms of which it is composed, and to discover exactly how it is put together. Its findings and achievements demand our most careful attention, and every effort should be made to put them to practical use. At the same time that this type of minute analysis proceeds, we must also seek to foster, it seems to me, an overall insight that can comprehend mankind, and indeed all forms of life, as a whole. This requires synthesis rather than analysis.

The men of ancient Greece and India exercised that kind of insight in their attempts to explain the world around them. They asserted that the world is made up of four basic elements, earth, water, fire, and wind, and they further believed that man himself is constituted of the very same elements. This was the essential view held in both East and West, though to these four basic elements the men of the East in their wisdom added a fifth, the element of space or emptiness.

In the eyes of modern science, which has isolated and identified over a hundred different elements, such a view may seem hopelessly primitive. And yet the point we must not fail to note is that this view sees man as made of the same essential stuff as the universe and attempts to relate his existence to the larger dimensions of the universe as a whole, surely a keen philosophical perceptiveness and anything but primitive. That this view prevailed in both East and West may indicate the degree to which Eastern ways of thought influenced Greek culture, but in any event we can only marvel at the wide acceptance which it enjoyed among men of ancient times.

The concept of the five elements of earth, water, fire, wind, and space was not, like the concepts of modern science, based upon materialistic modes of thought. Rather it derived from the view that man and the universe constitute a single harmonious entity. Consequently, sickness occurs because of some lack of harmony among these basic elements as they exist in man, while death represents the return of these elements to their original source in the universe.

It would be no exaggeration to say that the human body contains within it all the rhythms of the universe. And in fact, as medical science has shown, in the daytime the heartbeat quickens, the blood pressure rises, and the cells of the brain become highly active. When night comes, the process is reversed, the blood pressure lowers, and the heart begins to beat less rapidly. Thus the rhythms of the universe are matched in almost uncanny fashion by those of the human body. For all we know, the elements of earth, water, fire, wind, and space within the body may be responding to their counterparts in the universe and carrying on subtle movements in harmony with one another. In any event, my teacher used to urge me to be in bed by midnight, a piece of advice I have always found to be wise.

Built into each living organism there is something like a timepiece, which keeps it in rhythm with the movements of the earth, the sun, the moon, and the other components of the universe. The study of this principle, called biorhythm in modern terminology, constitutes a new field of research which attempts to view man as a harmonious entity whose rhythms are related to those of the natural world.

Western man in ancient times claimed to see the gods and heroes of his mythology embodied in the constellations. This, I venture to think, was not done out of any simple desire to lend mystery to the stars. Rather it was based upon a wish to understand his gods better and thereby to discover some way in which to predict the influences they would exert on the world of human affairs. In traditional Chinese thought the mythological element was largely circumvented and the actual movements of the stars themselves were looked upon as governing human destiny.

The universe, for all its vastness and complexity, throbs with movement like a single beautiful living entity. And man, who exists as an inescapable part of it, constitutes a model in miniature of the universe. To perceive the true nature of man and to discover how human life and human society can be brought to a state of perfect harmony—these are the essential points to which the wisdom of man must be directed, the crux of the problem before us.

THE LEGACY
OF ANCIENT TIMES

I love the area around Nara. In comparison to our big modern cities, which year by year seem to lose more of the old-fashioned Japanese warmth and sensitivity, its villages retain a rare aura of poetry, something of the rich lyric feeling of the *Man'yōshū*, the great anthology of early Japanese verse compiled in Nara in the eighth century.

This is the region known as the land of Yamato. In the seventh and eighth centuries it produced the vigorous and striking works of art associated with the Hakuhō and Tempyō eras. It is the birthplace of Asuka culture, the first great era in Japanese cultural history, and of its most revered representative, Prince Shōtoku, a statesman of sagacity and vision who in the seventh century encouraged the spread of Buddhism and continental learning in Japan.

And now we learn that, in the village of Asuka in this renowned region of Nara, a tomb dating from that ancient period and decorated with splendid murals has just been discovered. Suddenly we find ourselves in possession of a wonderful gift coming to us from our ancestors of over a thousand years ago, the men who created that far-off culture of Asuka times. This news, like a spring breeze, brings joy to the heart.

Discovered in March of 1972, the Takamatsu Tomb, as it is known, has become the focus of enormous excitement and debate. The color reproductions of the murals in newspapers and magazines show a brilliance and freshness that make it all but impossible to believe they date from the late sixth or early seventh century, the date tentatively assigned to them by scholars. A well-known Japanese style painter, who has been appointed to make copies of the murals, reports that he is at a loss to know what

126

sort of pigments could have been employed to produce such marvelous hues.

Simple as the paintings are in design, they have a vitality and lingering fragrance suggestive of the warmth of living flesh. The figures, most of them women, are dressed in costumes unlike those of ancient Japan, long flowing robes of elegant design. This perhaps indicates that the wearers are immigrants from the continent. The gentle postures of the women with their rounded, rouge-touched cheeks bring to mind an ancient scene of rustic tranquility, and I seem to see them strolling among the grasses and trees of the village of Asuka.

> *With a basket, pretty basket,*
> *a trowel, pretty trowel,*
> *maiden digging herbs on the hillside,*
> *may I ask where you live?*

So begins the poem by Emperor Yūryaku, the first work in the *Man'yōshū*. It was a time when even emperors spoke in a simple and unaffected manner, and the figures in the Takamatsu murals convey to me the same feeling, so appropriate to this homeland of the *Man'yōshū*. At the same time they seem to offer a wordless but poignant plea to those of us today, rushing about on our endless frantic errands, to revive once again the spirit of poetry in our hearts.

There is another thing about the Takamatsu burial chamber I find particularly intriguing. That is the diagram of the heavenly bodies incised on the ceiling of the chamber, the sun inset with gold foil, the stars with silver foil, and vermilion lines connecting one star to another. It is, I am told, a representation of the constellations, and was used by the men of ancient times as a calendar.

According to this ancient system of astronomy, the vast dome of the heavens was divided up into twenty-eight constellations. By observing the positions of these constellations and of the sun and moon, men attempted to determine the days, months, and seasons of the year. The twenty-eight divisions were known as the Twenty-eight Mansions, seven of them being assigned to each of the four directions. The wisdom of ancient man, it would seem, had taught him how to converse with the stars and to measure his movements by theirs. There is strong evidence to indicate that the system originated in India and was later adopted in China, from whence it passed to the islands of Japan. The design of the constellations was probably placed in the burial chamber to serve as a map for the dead man, representing the new world to which he would go. Arranged on the flat ceiling of the chamber, it presents a beautiful geometric diagram of the stars, as one would see them winking in the night sky when he gazed upward into the dome of the heavens. According to one scholar, this is the largest diagram of the constellations so far found in the world.

The system of the twenty-eight constellations is related to the lunar calendar. Whether one is speaking of the lunar or of the solar calendar, it seems to me that this custom of using the movements of heavenly bodies as the basis upon which to construct a calendar for human activities indicates a deep desire on the part of man to harmonize the pace and direction of his daily movements with those of the universe.

If even the jumble and confusion of daily human pursuits could be brought into agreement with the eternal and unvarying rhythms of the heavens, then one could create his own miniature version of the order of the universe. Was this the view of life that led men to construct their calendars in this fashion? Or was it a realization that even the movements of the celestial bodies are indelibly a part of the fundamental rhythm of human life? Perhaps this is also what led the men of ancient times to look upon apparent irregularities in the movements of the heavenly bodies as omens of irregularity and disruption in human society. In China and other countries where the system of the twenty-eight constellations was adopted, dislocations in that system were looked upon as a type of calamity having dire implications for the welfare of man.

Such views of the interrelatedness of man and the universe would be dismissed today as absurd nonsense. And yet present-day science is even now in the process of demonstrating to us how much more sensitive and complex the human body is than even the most delicate machine.

Anyone can recall in general the things that happened to him yesterday, though it may be difficult to remember all the details. As days turn into months and months into years, however, such memories become increasingly dim. Yet medical science assures us that not the slightest particle is ever erased from the mind; it is only that we lose the power to call up

128

memories at will. Certainly everyone is familiar with the way something he thought he had completely forgotten may, because of some chance circumstance, suddenly come to mind again. And we often hear stories of how a person facing death or some other imminent catastrophe will see all the events of his past life flash before his mind like the figures on a revolving lantern.

With perhaps some degree of exaggeration, we may say that, through the power of memory, all the events that have occurred within the experience of the individual, including even the movements of the heavenly bodies, have become indelibly etched upon his spirit. We may go even a step farther and speculate that somewhere within his unconscious lie memories of the experiences of his parents, or of the entire past history of mankind from the time when human life began, transmitted to him through his genetic makeup.

I recall reading somewhere that the number of possible combinations of brain cells within the human mind exceeds the number of atoms in the entire universe. If so, does the mind then perhaps have the potential to follow the movements of each and every one of those atoms?

If we stop to think of it, we may say that both the unlimited vastness of the universe and the eternal flow of time are miraculously condensed within the life of a single individual. If the men of ancient times perceived the motions of the heavenly bodies as an indispensible part of the rhythm of human life, and for that reason drew their diagrams of the dome of heaven with its twenty-eight constellations as a map of the world to which the dead man would soon belong, we can only be filled with renewed admiration for their keen intuitive wisdom. And we can feel nothing but shame for the shallowness of modern man who, bound by petty egoism and his preoccupation with what lies immediately before his eyes, makes no effort to explore the treasures of this wonderful life force by which he is bound directly to the universe itself.

As research progresses, the newly discovered Takamatsu Tomb will no doubt provide us with a rich fund of information concerning the daily life of ancient man and his spiritual beliefs. One of the most important functions of archeology, it seems to me, is to rediscover through its investigations the rich and varied wisdom of the men of the past, wisdom that has been discarded or forgotten by the men of the present.

The essential pains and joys of human life do not change even in the course of a thousand years. And it follows that the wisdom men evolved in their efforts to cope with life must be founded upon a common ground, whether they belong to the past or the present. The Takamatsu Tomb, a glorious cultural legacy from our predecessors of the distant past, fills us with a sense of pride and possession we have not known for a long time. The question now is how, by using it as an impetus for self-reflection, we can best come to appreciate its true meaning and worth.

THE HOUSEWIFE
IN SOCIETY

The season has come when, on more and more mornings, you find you can see your breath when you get up. At night the sharp sound of footsteps on the pavement and the little shrunken moon convey a feeling of indescribable cold. As people rush about busily, you have a sense of the winter season marching inexorably toward you, the cold increasing with each step.

It is the time for settling up the household accounts for the year that is drawing to a close and planning the budget for next year, a time when the housewife is the true master of the family. The younger children are busy enjoying their winter vacation, brief though it is, while the husbands, those "older children" of the family, are off to a round of parties celebrating the close of the old year and the start of the new. Meanwhile, the housewives are expected to tend to a thousand and one matters, holding things together at home, tidying up year-end business, and extending the season's greetings to friends, relatives and neighbors. Some of them with particularly lazy husbands are even burdened with the additional task of writing and sending off New Year's greeting cards.

People talk about the need to do away with empty formalities, but I think there is something very fine about the custom of exchanging New Year's cards and greetings. Though it may be no more than a simple postcard, a greeting card can convey news of a dear friend far away, or may serve to revive a friendship that has meant much to one in the past. Formalities observed solely out of a sense of duty surely have little worth. The solution, however, is not to abolish them, it seems to me, but to find some way to restore true meaning to them.

New Year's is a time for deepening and strengthening the ties that bind people to one another. In our present society, when human relations tend so often to become arid, it serves as an invaluable oasis, and for that reason the greetings and other customs of the New Year's season help to restore warmth to human ties and deserve to be prized and carried on.

Japan is a small country jam-packed with people. Europeans and Americans often remark that they have a feeling of suffocation just from looking at our crowded cities, our trains packed with commuters, and our little houses crammed together without lawns around them, too small to allow each of the occupants to have a room of his own. They even say they admire the Japanese for being able to live under such crowded conditions. It's not a situation we can feel very happy about. But one thing is certain —under such circumstances, unless we can make certain that human relations are conducted in a smooth and mutually satisfactory manner, we can never hope to build a harmonious society. In many cases, several families live under a single roof, with only a single wall dividing them. If they have no concern for each others' living habits and preferences, or are actively hostile toward each other, they can never expect their own family life to proceed smoothly. And it is even less likely that they will make any positive contribution to the community in which they live.

Recently I heard of a case where neighbors quarreled because one said that the other's wind-bell made too much noise! Some people may ask how a little bell tinkling in the wind could possibly be so annoying, while others may point out that if the sound is loud enough, it can be a first-rate nuisance. However that may be, one cannot help feeling downcast at the fact that such a trivial matter should become the cause of contention between neighbors. If people living side by side are so lacking in mutual understanding that they could quarrel over trifles of this kind, it is clear that the families of the community have virtually ceased to have any meaningful contact with one another.

Our present-day society, in which people live jammed together and yet have almost no friendly human contact with each other, fills me with a sense of unspeakable coldness. Families who are forever bickering with one another are a decided improvement over those who simply shut themselves off from society behind walls of indifference. And I am deeply saddened when I hear of people resorting to law suits because of some complaint against their neighbors. People who would consider it proper to take such action could never be expected to play any significant part in improving the life of the community.

Japanese people love festivals. Most festivals are religious in nature, though some of them seem more like tourist attractions. Their origins, however, are to be found in very simple, basic instincts. In olden times in Japan, the farmers and their families were so busy planting the spring crops and reaping the autumn harvest that they had no time to enjoy themselves. But when the work was over, they would gather at some public place such as a shrine or temple and hold a festival to celebrate the harvest. In a sense, it was an indication of the poverty in which the people lived, for they could not afford to feast and celebrate in such a fashion more than once, or at best two or three times, in the course of a year. At the same time, it suggests what great importance the villagers attached to the matter of human relations.

Over the centuries, festivals have fostered in the Japanese people their sense of community solidarity. In recent years in modern housing projects and apartment complexes the old festival instinct has manifested itself in a new form, giving rise to the so-called people's plazas, which are designed to encourage community spirit. If such places can help to promote more friendly relations among the members of the community and give them a deeper sense of unity, then they will have played a very meaningful role indeed. It will be a splendid thing if these activities do not remain simply a yearly occurrence, but become a regular part of daily life, and if they go beyond mere festive celebration and lead to open and serious exchanges of opinion. It is the housewives of the community who play the crucial role in these activities, and they are the ones I look to to make such activities a success.

I have always thought that women should not shut themselves up in their homes, and have frequently appealed to them not to do so. I know that they have many things to do around the house, and certainly there are no concerns more important than child raising and education. But if for that reason women cut themselves off from social contacts, concern themselves only with family matters, and give no thought to the community around them, then I believe they will never be able to expand their knowledge and vision.

I have heard that the average housewife in Japan spends something like five hours a day watching television. I can assure you that bit of information came as a shock to me. Now that most homes have electrical appliances of various kinds, the time required to do housework has been greatly shortened. But if the hours thus freed are spent simply watching TV, then I would have to conclude that women in Japan are deliberately shutting themselves up and failing to get out of the house even when they have the opportunity. When I visualize a housewife glued to a television screen during the midday hours, and then in the late afternoon and evening, when the children have come home from school, continuing to sit and stare at the machine, I feel very depressed.

I am not saying that watching television in itself is bad. If TV serves to arouse an interest in society and social problems, then watching it can be a worthwhile experience. But if one reduces the viewing time by two or three hours a day, and develops the habit of getting out of the house during that time, how much more worthwhile the experience could be. One can talk over with one's neighbors the things one has seen and been impressed by on television and can help them to become more aware of social problems. By doing so, it seems to me, one can improve one's own understanding and consciousness and at the same time play a part in bettering the community.

As soon as one begins talking about playing a role in the community, many women tend to shrink away. They seem to think that in order to do so, they must neglect their families or their personal interests, or that they must involve themselves in some large-scale political or social movement. This attitude strikes me as highly mistaken.

In times past, it is true, there has been a persistent belief that one could make a significant contribution to society only at the cost of some kind of personal sacrifice. A number of those who have made such a contribution in the past have in fact sacrificed their own interests, and in some cases even their lives. We think of them as very noble. How fine, how beautiful a thing it is to forget oneself and give one's all for others! But if contributing to society is such a difficult undertaking, then we are likely to conclude that only a small number of people are capable of doing so.

People are basically self-centered. We may say that the instinct to survive forces them to be that way. Even if told to rid themselves of their egoism, the great majority of people could not do so. What is important, I think, is for people to come to understand that looking after their own interests means looking after the concerns of the group as a whole, and that to contribute to the group is to insure one's own protection and well-being.

A truism, you may say. But it is precisely because it is so true that it becomes important to repeat it. No family can exist apart from the society around it, but no family can hope to contribute to society unless it is a happy, harmoniously functioning unit in itself. Excessive attention to personal interests will not do, nor will too much emphasis upon self-sacrifice.

Buddhism teaches that all one's actions will invariably come back to confront one in the end. The principle is known as the law of cause and effect and holds that a good action will call forth a good result, a bad one a bad result. In recent years, with the worsening of environmental pollution, we have seen striking evidence of the working of that law in the world of natural science. People dumped contaminated wastes into the ocean, believing they would have no harmful effect. But the pollution was absorbed by plankton, the plankton was eaten by little fish, which were in turn eaten by larger fish, and when the larger fish were caught and consumed by human beings, the pollution found its way back to its source. The same process was duplicated in rivers and lakes as well. Advances in the study of ecology have shown us that the natural world is an unending cycle, that all of its aspects are intimately related one to another.

Not only the natural world, but the world of human society too, is made up of similarly interrelated parts. No matter what walls and fences we erect in an effort to isolate ourselves from the rest of society, we still remain a part of the overall cycle. If in thinking only of our own personal interests we dump our wastes upon society, as it were, it is clear that they will come back to plague us in the end.

In Buddhist teaching, one often encounters the saying, "Those who laugh at the good keepers of the precepts will meet with the king's punishment." Translated into modern day language, it means that those who despise or make fun of others who are taking a leading role in society and contributing to it in significant ways will find themselves rejected by society and denied its protection. It may seem a rather understated example of cause and effect, but it points up how intimate is the connection between the individual and society, and how the actions of the individual will return to haunt him.

By citing the example of a material substance, the pollution mentioned above, we have indicated how all the different parts of the natural world are interrelated. And in the immaterial realms of the spirit, of social goals and values, we must understand that this quality of interrelatedness exists, exerting an influence that is perhaps even more pervasive than that of the environmental pollution we have discussed. Society is a highly complex organism, not subject to simple analyses and explanations, so let me give an example of the kind of interrelatedness I mean. Suppose someone displays an attitude of contempt toward another person. The person who has been treated with contempt will react with anger and will speak ill of the person who scorned him. The process will repeat itself until the person who initiated it eventually finds himself shunned and disliked by everyone around him. Anyone who concerns himself solely with selfish aims will discover that in the end he is the one who suffers. On the other hand, a person who shows respect for others will in time come to be respected, and will help to encourage respect for others among society as a whole.

Though on the surface it may appear that in urging the importance of consideration for others, I am preaching a doctrine of self-sacrifice, there is one basic difference to be noted. It is the fact that, by helping to contribute to the welfare of others, one is in reality demonstrating respect and concern for himself.

When parents show a concern for society as a whole, that in itself will exercise an important influence upon the way they educate their children. A friend of mine has told me that each day he makes it a point to inform his children about world affairs and to discuss such affairs with them. (How like him, I thought.) Children brought up in that manner will undoubtedly play an important role in the future. It is my fervent hope, therefore, that such an attitude and approach will become common in society, and particularly among housewives, who exercise such a crucial influence in the home education of their children.

GLASS CHILDREN

It's always good to see New Year's come around. Though one's reaction to it may be slightly different depending upon whether one is young or old, a woman or a man, still amidst the festivity there is a sense of mental tidying up and a renewal of deep emotions. And in particular, as one watches the little children racing around in delightful play, one spontaneously utters a prayer that the new year will be a good one for them.

At such a season, it is nice to go downtown with the whole family and enjoy the holiday atmosphere, and it is also nice just to sit at home with the pleasure of each other's company. Every channel on the TV is featuring some special holiday program in a scramble to attract viewers. At such a time when I am relaxing with my family, I always think how fine it would be if we had some folktales that we could tell to each other. Something, perhaps, like Tolstoy's *Ivan the Fool*. If only stories like that were told in families everywhere, the cold, unfriendly world we live in today, I am sure, would become a much warmer and pleasanter place. There is something in the immortal story of Ivan that even now speaks to us with great power and appeal.

Many of you probably know the story already. Ivan is the youngest of three sons of a prosperous farm family in a certain country. Just below him in age is a little sister who has been dumb from birth. The oldest brother is a soldier. He is married to a woman of aristocratic birth, relies on military might in all things, and is filled with a desire to dominate others. The second brother has a big potbelly and thinks of nothing but money. His aim is always to turn a profit, no matter what comes along.

137

Ivan, by contrast, dresses in rags and doesn't know how to do anything but take care of his little sister and work away silently and doggedly in the fields.

The story tells how an old devil and three little devils get together and devise various schemes to sow dissension among the three brothers and drive them to ruin. The story is told with great humor and abounds in simple moral lessons. The two older brothers, as it turns out, eventually fall victim to the devils' evil schemes, but not Ivan. The temptations of power, the seductions of money, all the devices the devils can conjure up prove utterly ineffective against him, and their thirty-six strategies collapse in failure. It is Ivan the Fool who in the end is the victor.

Ivan is indeed a fool. Everything he does is motivated by complete and artless honesty. No matter how others may try to cheat him, he never grows angry, but with a boundless magnanimity simply says, "Oh, don't do that!" He is the kind who was born to forgive others. And above all he has patience, planting his feet firmly on the earth when difficulties threaten, gripping the plow with his calloused hands, and never letting go. He is a figure who in stature far surpasses the heroes of ordinary didactic tales.

A character like this, who would never dream of becoming disheartened over any little trial or tribulation, has few counterparts in the Japanese tradition. Of course, he is symbolic of the battle that Tolstoy in his old age waged against the vanity and affectation of modern civilization. But I think he also represents a quality that is becoming increasingly rare in our time. Education, I believe we would all agree, should not be an activity that forces children into a mold dictated by the demands of society, turning out adults who are timorous and stereotyped in their behavior. Rather it should foster the qualities of perseverance and great-mindedness, the confidence to keep pushing forward on the path one has chosen. It should foster, in other words, the simple honesty and directness personified in the figure of Ivan.

These days I am constantly pained by reports of children committing suicide, running away from home or developing serious cases of neurosis. Japan is already in danger of losing its vitality, its spirit, and the trust of the rest of the world. Must our own children now turn away from us in this tragic way, so that we lose our future as well? Has the failure of the

138

nation's adults cast a shadow over the children, so that when the adults try to draw near them, they dart aside and like so many lemmings dash headlong to their death? What causes me the most heartache is the fragility of the children of today. They seem to be made of glass. They have no toughness. They're so weak you expect them at any moment to break. It is easy enough to blame society or the adult world. But doing so will not restore the future hope of the nation. We must begin the painful process of finding out just what is wrong and how it can be corrected.

What has made the children so weak? What has taught them to run away from life? What is the cause, and how can it be remedied? It is the duty of the adults of today to answer these bitter questions, not with pretty words and facile phrases but with solid sense, not evasively but with a frank and challenging attitude.

An educational expert has told me that the children in recent years have become very clumsy at using their hands. There are few children who know how to handle a pair of scissors or a knife. They of course don't have to sharpen their pencils with a knife, as children used to do, because the electric pencil sharpener does it for them. They don't have to use a pair of scissors when they want to make something, because they can buy plastic model kits in which the pieces are ready-made. There is no doubt that the conveniences of modern life, by taking the place of human hands and feet, have robbed our children of the tools they used to use.

But the educational expert also told me that one of the main reasons the children don't know how to handle a knife or a pair of scissors is that their mothers won't allow them to handle such things. The mothers claim they cannot do otherwise, since the children might injure themselves. So if the child wants to eat a piece of fruit, mother peels it for him.

No one would deny that knives and scissors can be dangerous. But it is one thing to protect a child from danger and another for the mother to do every last thing for her child. The educational expert told me that when he sees a child who has never peeled a piece of fruit for himself, he feels not so much pity for the child as anger at the overprotectiveness of the parents.

Children are not born weak. Of course, human babies cannot stand on their two legs immediately after birth the way the young of some animals can. But it is reported that, with a little training, a newborn baby is capable of swimming. And even without training, it is clear that the baby has the strength needed to swim. This shows that even a newly born infant has plenty of innate capabilities. I am of course not saying that one should actually make babies swim. I do believe, however, there is a real danger that the habit of reliance fostered through too much protectiveness can dull the capabilities inherent in the child, deprive him of his strength, and make it impossible for him to learn to swim in the river of life.

While this may sound like a rather blunt way to put it, it seems to me that in many cases, it is not that the children are naturally clumsy, but that they have been made clumsy by the parents. Perhaps the advances of science and technology are making the whole human race clumsy. How many people these days own tools for making things by hand?

As I recall, when I was a child I was never without a bump or a cut of some kind. Most of the time I helped with the family business rather than playing children's games, but I was always making something or jumping around in the mud, and you may be sure I had as many bruises and injuries as the next child. Those were hard times, when people had to make all kinds of things for themselves, and that necessity taught the children the wisdom and courage required to get through life.

But I wonder what the mothers of today are doing to instill wisdom and courage in their children. When children reach a certain age, why not teach them how to use a knife or a pair of scissors? Naturally, one has to take care at the same time that they don't injure themselves. But if a parent doesn't do that much, and instead insists upon doing all the cutting and scissoring for the child, he or she is in a sense guilty of foolish overprotectiveness.

Scissors or knives are in themselves no very serious problem. What is serious is the habit of dependence nurtured by not letting the child use them. If a child is frightened by every little wave that comes along, running away from the waves or expecting someone else to face them for him, then when he goes forth to face the great ocean of life, he will be helpless and terrified. I suppose that is why we see mothers going along with their children when the latter take their college entrance exams or exams to enter company employment. But what will happen when these young people, who are half child and half adult, face some big wave that they cannot run away from and that no one can face for them? When I hear of a child committing suicide, I always think I hear the voice of a drowning child crying for help, a child who has never been taught to swim.

Children must be given the strength to live and fight for themselves. "If you love your child, send him on a journey," the saying goes. And people in olden times actually did send their children on journeys. There is nothing that fills a parent with greater anxiety or forlornness than sending a child off on a trip alone. And yet parents in bygone days forced themselves to do so.

I wonder if parents today could bear to do the same? Or could they even bear to help the child day by day to build the strength and ability to journey through life alone? Are they not in fact doing just the opposite, in the morning depriving the child of the strength of his hands, in the evening taking away the strength of his legs, at noon shielding him from the burning rays of the sun, at night protecting him from the cold wind, so that the child must remain forever dependent upon the parent? A child brought up in this manner, if he one day should venture out into the open sunlight, will collapse before the severity of the elements. If a parent has let a child have his way and has never taught him the patience needed to do homework, then the parent must bear the responsibility if the child commits suicide in despair because he cannot get through the homework assigned him for the summer vacation.

Suppose a little child falls down on the street. The parent who rushes over to embrace him, saying, "There, there, it's all right!" I would put in the lowest category. Even a parent who shows no concern whatsoever and leaves the child entirely to his own devices is an improvement. The true parent is somewhere in between, worrying about the child, but at the same time teaching him to pick himself up by his own efforts.

I have been in just such a position myself many times in the past. And I have noticed something interesting. A child who has fallen down no doubt feels some degree of pain. He screws up his face as though getting ready to cry, but at the same time he looks at the parent's face. In other words, though he is in pain, he will look around first to try to determine whether he should cry or not. If someone says, "Oh dear, that must have hurt!" he will instantly burst into a flood of tears. But if he hears, "Big boys don't cry!" you may be fairly certain that he won't. Of course, children vary greatly and one can't lay down any general rules, but in this situation I think you will find that the reaction is fairly uniform.

I have spoken of one particular situation, and yet I believe that the reaction of the parent in that one moment can make an indelible impression on the child's character. It is a minor incident, but not one to be lightly dismissed. As such minor incidents recur again and again, they shape the whole direction of the child's life.

You may ask how I have brought up my own three sons. I would have to reply that, being so busy with other things, I am afraid I have been rather neglectful of their home education. Still, after years of dashing around in our small house, they have somehow managed to grow up; the oldest is twenty-four, the second twenty-two, and the third nineteen. They are all different in personality. The eldest is on the intellectual side, the second is very lively and cheerful. The third is a perfectionist who has somehow managed to evade pressure and interference from his older brothers and goes very much his own way. Since his elementary school days he has had a passion for astronomical observation. At the moment he is off with his friends in the Ogasawara Islands south of Tokyo, where the skies are very clear at night. He also seems to have fisherman's blood in him, as he loves the sea and is completely at home on it. In college he has joined the ocean sailing club, and as soon as vacation comes around, he is off to Aburatsubo in Kanagawa Prefecture for sailing. As a consequence, I hardly ever see him.

One day in May of last year, he went out with his friends for training in a sailboat on a morning when the sea was rather rough. When they got off Irōzaki Peninsula, a sudden wind came up and the boat capsized. On top of that, the motorboat that was supposed to come to their rescue developed engine trouble. They were finally picked up by a passing ship. Meanwhile, my son and his friends did what they could to encourage each other and keep their spirits up. When he got home, he pretended nothing had happened. It was only when my wife remarked that he seemed to be coming down with a cold that the story finally came out.

I knew nothing at all about the affair at the time; I heard about it later from my wife. I was not so much surprised as I was impressed by the singlemindedness with which young people throw themselves into their activities. My wife was worried, but as she remarked, she would rather

142

have him out on the ocean getting toughened up than playing around in dubious parts of the city. I am no different from other parents, so of course I breathed a sigh of relief that nothing bad had happened. At the same time I couldn't help smiling to think that my son had grown up with such independence of character.

I have never merely stared down at my children from above. Nor have I ever demanded that they watch me all the time. I have hoped only that they would fix their gaze on social justice, that far-off goal upon which I keep my own eyes fixed, and that they would do so naturally and not because they were forced to. The "education" I have given them perhaps amounts to no more than that. We have not been a family who spent a lot of time conferring with one another. Still, I have always hoped we would be a family who keeps looking in the direction of the same distant range of mountains. The road I walk along my children will walk along too, and their children in turn, each generation advancing farther upon it. In this way, I believe, a golden road created by tireless human effort can be opened up.

It may appear from what I have said so far that my view of children's education is lacking in one important aspect. That is, it fails to inquire what the purpose of education is. I would like therefore to propose as the basic aim of education the slogan, "Education for the sake of self-reliance." Children are not the property of the parents. They are independent individuals, individuals who have not yet acquired their full strength. Because they are as yet lacking in strength, one must take care of them. And because they are independent individuals, one must teach them self-reliance.

The Japanese word for education is *kyōiku*. The element *iku* means "to raise." In spring, one plants seeds, and from the seeds plants grow up. Men clear away the weeds and give the plants fertilizer. But it is the plants themselves that take in the fertilizer from the soil. Raising the plants means guarding them and their surroundings so that they can stand up by themselves and become self-reliant. And for that reason the element *kyō* of *kyōiku*, which means "to teach," must mean to teach the quality of self-reliance.

If one makes the teaching of self-reliance the goal of children's education, then the educational methods best suited for achieving that goal

143

will become apparent of themselves. At one time, there was much discussion as to whether one should use Spartan methods in raising children or raise them by the laissez-faire method. Both have much to be said for them, and for a time public opinion seems to have been divided on the question. But this was no more than a debate over methods. It is unfortunate that some people seem to have mistaken it for a debate over goals.

The goal, as I have said, should at all times be self-reliance. In order to inculcate self-reliance, strict training will at times be necessary, while at other times it will be imperative to let the child follow his own way. Generally speaking, strict discipline will be best applied in the years before the child reaches the age of discretion. As the child grows older, he should be left more and more to exercise his independent judgment on how to behave.

In actual practice, however, one finds all too often that just the opposite course is adopted. While the child is little, he is consistently spoiled by the parents and allowed to do just as he pleases. Then, later, a sudden and frantic effort is made to teach him to mind. By that time it is too late. A child will never develop a sense of self-reliance under such circumstances.

Children may be small, but they have a great capacity to absorb things. An amount of learning that would take an adult any number of years to acquire, a child can absorb in a day, a month, or a year. And because the child's mind is not cluttered with previous information, the newly learned material will stick in his mind and be difficult to expunge.

Children are interested in anything and everything. Their interest is indiscriminate. The parents can respond to these displays of interest in various ways. They may listen carefully to what the child has to say or they may show indifference; they may encourage the child's interests or they may restrain them.

In this way, a process of selection begins to take place in the child's mind. And those interests that meet with restraint from the parent will be inhibited in their development. In this way the child's personality is formed. Of course, the child himself will possess certain inherited traits and tendencies. But the influence which the parent exercises upon the child is also of incalculable importance.

If the child is to become self-reliant, he must be given strength and power. He must be given the power that comes with knowledge and the power that comes with skill. And in order to do this, an effort must be made to develop his innate talents. Of course, not all these can be developed to perfection, but efforts must be made to develop them to the highest degree possible.

I would stress that, in order to awaken the child's vitality, to uncover the buds of his talent and nourish them in the sun, the child must be provided with surroundings rich in interest and challenge, so that in such an atmosphere he may learn to move ahead on his own.

When education is oriented toward the development of self-reliance, discipline will come to have a somewhat different meaning. It will cease to consist merely of negative injunctions not to do this or that. On the contrary, it will of necessity come to embody a positive approach that teaches the child the correct way to proceed. Thus, for example, if the child has been doing something to cause annoyance or inconvenience to others, it is not enough simply to scold him. He should be made to go in person and apologize to the person he has been troubling. In this way he can be trained in time to move according to the dictates of his own conscience.

I began this essay by talking about New Year's customs and have somehow ended up on the subject of child education. But there is a connection, since New Year's is the beginning of the year, and childhood is the beginning of life. In all affairs, it is the initial stage that is most important. We must keep that always in mind.

This year, as always, various New Year's ceremonies and celebrations will be conducted in many places. In saying our prayers for the coming year, let us not look to fearful demons or gods of good luck to frighten or cajole us into diligence. Let us pray rather for a society in which diligence will be dictated by the religious faith and conviction of the individual, in which one does not look to others for favors but rather seeks to do one's best for others. If all of us, adults and children alike, make that our prayer, then this will be a truly festive occasion.

MY DEFINITION
OF HAPPINESS

People do not live in isolation. Dwelling in the nexus of family, society, and the world of nature, they lend support to one another. Happiness likewise does not exist as an isolated quality, nor does it conform to a single fixed pattern. Human happiness is something that breathes and has its being in the relationships between one person and another.

I recall a very engaging story I once read about the love between husband and wife, O. Henry's "The Gift of the Magi." I hope those of you who are familiar with it will pardon me if I outline the story here.

It concerns a young married couple named Della and Jim, who are poor and live in a furnished flat for which they pay eight dollars a week. It is the day before Christmas and the husband and wife have been considering what gifts to give each other as an expression of their devotion. The wife, Della, wants to give her husband a watch chain to go with the gold watch he inherited from his grandfather and of which he is very proud. She finds that the chain costs $21.00, and all she has is $1.87. She decides that the only thing to do is to sell her beautiful brown hair, which is so long it reaches to her knees. East or West, a woman's hair, it would seem, means as much as life itself to her. But Della makes the sacrifice, selling the hair to a wigmaker, and with the money buys a platinum watch chain. Her heart pounding with excitement, she waits for her husband to come home. He returns at last, and when he sees her, he is dumbfounded. The present he has brought home for his dear wife is a pair of tortoiseshell combs to wear in her beautiful hair.

Della assures him that her hair will grow long again in no time, and holds out her hand with the platinum watch chain gleaming in it. Jim collapses on the couch, then says with a smile, "Dell, let's put our Christmas presents away and keep 'em a while. They're too nice to use just at present. I sold the watch to get the money to buy your combs."

The little story, told with humor and pathos, in a most appealing way demonstrates, through the gifts the couple give one another, just how deep is the love between husband and wife.

Each has sacrificed something very dear in order to buy a suitable present. But when they present their gifts, they discover that there is no longer a gold watch to attach the chain to, and no longer any beautiful brown hair to wear the tortoiseshell combs in. Both gifts have turned out to be useless to them. A practical-minded young couple of today would probaby point out that if the husband and wife had only discussed beforehand what they were going to give each other, they could have spared themselves the waste. But the story deals with something that far transcends that kind of calculating and logic. It concerns the beauty of the true love of husband and wife. In demonstrating their love for one another, the pair find that in fact they have given each other a priceless gift, which is why the story is entitled "The Gift of the Magi." It deals, in other words, with the freely giving nature of love.

As I write these words, I am suddenly reminded of Dr. and Mrs. Arnold J. Toynbee. Dr. Toynbee passed away several years ago, but his wife Veronica, now eighty-three or eighty-four, I believe is living alone quietly somewhere in the city of York. In May of 1972, and again in May of the following year, I had occasion to stay at the Toynbee home, where Dr. Toynbee and I carried out discussions for a period of five days on each occasion.

We customarily began our discussions at ten in the morning. In a room next to Dr. Toynbee's study, we sat on a sofa, our backs to the window, and talked. Soon the bright May sun shining through the windowpane would begin to make the room quite warm. Mrs. Toynbee, who sat in a chair a little way apart, would then get up and open the window for us. There was a park close by, and the sound of birds singing would drift in on the clear morning air. In an atmosphere of calm and quiet we would carry on our earnest conversations.

After an hour or so had passed, Mrs. Toynbee would get up to make some Japanese green tea. Sipping the tea, we would shed our earlier feeling of tension and speak in a more relaxed mood. Mrs. Toynbee seldom moved about while the discussions were going on. She sat listening to us, the gentle expression never leaving her face. On rare occasions, she might offer her husband a word of advice, but she never tried to interpose in the discussion. She was restrained in her remarks, seeming if anything to be on the reticent side. On the other hand, there was nothing gloomy or withdrawn about her. She was dressed simply and gave an impression of great refinement and intellectual depth.

Dr. Toynbee told me a little about how he had met his wife and about their early married life and work together, though I never attempted to press him for details. On the other hand, since I spent a total of ten days or so with them, I could not help but observe and sense many things about them as a couple. If I were to sum up my observations, I would say that I do not believe Dr. Toynbee could in his late years have continued so clear in mind and bequeathed such a wealth of pertinent advice and warning to mankind if it had not been for the devoted support and care he received from his wife. When we held our discussions, he was already dependent upon a hearing aid; I believe his hearing had been failing for some time in the past. His wife acted as a pair of ears for him, conveying to him information that he could not hear himself. And more important, she not only relayed what she had heard but added a few words of explanation so that he could more readily grasp the meaning.

In fact, I doubt that Dr. Toynbee could have lived to the age he did if it had not been for his wife. He suffered a heart attack when he was seventy, and was told that he would never leave his bed again. But, as he himself told me, his wife devotedly nursed him back to health. The care she took of him apparently restored vitality to his spirit.

Mrs. Toynbee graduated from Cambridge, being one of the first women to receive a bachelor's degree from that university. She became an assistant in the historical research project carried on by Dr. Toynbee at Chatham House, a research institute for the study of international problems. She gathered historical data, scanned the newspapers, and did typing. When Dr. Toynbee was not at his study in Chatham House, he and his wife would walk in the park or remain at home together. They even fixed breakfast together, Dr. Toynbee helping to do the cooking and wash the dishes. He said he found the exercise was good for his health. Though I spent only a week or so with them, I could glimpse a very deep personal relationship between the couple, a kind of communion of hearts and minds that seemed to bind them together as they passed through the stages of life.

We speak of the love between husband and wife, but in fact it is a thing that takes a thousand different forms. Sometimes the husband may appear to outsiders to be impossibly domineering, yet the couple manage to get along with a surprising degree of harmony. On the other hand, there are not a few cases in which the wife seems to have her way in everything, but still an atmosphere of peace prevails. And then there are couples who, while going through the motions of living together, appear to have little or no bond of affection between them. But then you hear that, in the midst of their busy schedules, they somehow arrange once or twice a year to go out to dinner together, and that they cherish the memory of these rare occasions, and you can't help smiling to yourself.

It is not the outside appearance that matters. I always think to myself that, when a couple have shared the joys and sorrows of life over a long period of time, a deep tie grows up between them and it cannot be severed by any outside force. It is not the kind of open, direct love we see expressed by young couples. It is something not fully encompassed in the simple word "love," something broad and deep, representative of the power of a shared destiny. I have known some twenty or thirty elderly couples who seem to possess this power, and I have experienced the atmosphere of indescribable fullness and maturity that it creates. There is no suggestion about it either of regret or dissatisfaction. You will find among such couples none of the tedious and whining talk of some old people. And, although many of them have not lived easy lives by any means, you will not find in their expressions any hint of gloom. You will find only the sense of deep self-sufficiency that comes when two people have successfully made their way over life's rough places together, along with an awareness that the time is drawing near when they will most likely have to part.

I am reminded of the short story entitled *Jiisan Baasan* ("The Old Man and the Old Woman") by the Japanese novelist Mori Ōgai (1862–1922). It's beautifully written, and I expect many of you have read it. The story, if I may outline it in brief, goes something like this.

149

The time is the late Edo period, around the beginning of the nine-teenth century. An old man comes to take up residence in a little cottage on the grounds of an estate in Azabu Ryūdo-chō in Edo. He is reported to be the older brother of the owner of the estate. Though his hair is completely white, his bearing is dignified and his back unstooped by age. When two or three days have passed, an old woman appears and moves in with him. She too has white hair, done up in a neat bun, and is just as refined in manner and appearance as the old man. Happily fixing and eating their meals together, they appear like two little children playing house. They get along perfectly together, so perfectly, in fact, that the neighbors say that if they were a young couple, you could hardly have stood to watch them. At the same time, there is a kind of reserve and courtesy in their relations with each other; this leads to the rumor that they are in fact not husband and wife but brother and sister.

The author then goes on to describe their daily life in concise and telling language. "It was a carefree life they lived, one appropriate to an elderly couple in retirement. The old man would put on his glasses and read a book. Or he would write in a small hand in his diary. Each day at the same time, he would take out his sword, sprinkle polishing powder on it, and wipe it clean. He would also practice making passes with an imitation sword of wood. The old woman would be busy playing at housekeeping or, if she had a moment free, would sit down beside the old man and commence fanning him. It was the season when the weather is growing decidedly warm. After the old woman had fanned for a while, the old man would lay aside his book and begin talking. The two would talk as though they were having the best time in the world."

The old man's name, we learn, is Minobe Iori, age seventy-two. The old woman is his wife Run, age seventy-one. They married relatively late in life, when Iori was thirty and Run was twenty-nine. They had one child, a son. But while Run was pregnant with the child, Iori had to go on business to Kyoto. He had a great fondness for swords and, spotting a particularly fine specimen in a shop, he borrowed some money from an acquaintance and bought it. When the person from whom he borrowed the money appeared uninvited at a party where Iori was showing off his new sword, a quarrel arose between them. They drew their swords, and Iori fatally wounded the man. He was condemned to exile, and Run was obliged to take care of Iori's grandmother as well as her own newborn baby as best she could. In time the grandmother died, and her only child was carried off in a smallpox epidemic. But Run, steadfastly believing that her husband would return some day, went on bravely living. Meanwhile, thirty-seven years passed. Run, having heard that Iori had been pardoned at last, set out joyfully from her home in the Province of Awa, and the two were at last united.

The author spends no time probing the psychological makeup of his characters, nor does he give us any descriptions of the trials they underwent during their thirty-seven years of separation. And for that very reason, the harmony and affection that the old couple manifest after their reunion becomes more striking than ever. We can easily imagine wave after wave of hardships that confronted them. The author simply presents us with a couple in their old age, enjoying the feeling of satisfaction known only to those who have made their way through much difficulty, determined at all times never to be led astray by discontent or resentment. We are moved to admiration by the skill of the writer's presentation.

A true appreciation of happiness has something in common with the feelings of a man who, after a long period of confinement underground, at last emerges into the sunlight. He can appreciate the immense blessing of the sun's rays in a way quite impossible to someone who sees them day after day. Happiness is not, as some people suppose, a condition of calm and stability in which one is free from care. Rather it is the joy shared by a husband and wife who have successfully maneuvered their way through trouble and turmoil, a mutual joy binding their hearts together. A married life that proceeds smoothly and without difficulty, more or less by force of habit, may appear to be a happy one; in many cases it is in fact not happy at all. The important thing is not to escape trouble and hardship, but when it comes, to know how to face it without grumblings and mutual recriminations. When confronted with difficult circumstances, it is pointless to snap at those around one, or to turn backwards with a stream of complaints. The only wise course is to keep facing straight ahead and to consider first of all what one can do to overcome the difficulties.

One should never forget that the various kinds of tragedy that beset our society, the breakup of families, the ruptures between parents and children, ultimately are caused by ruptures within the human heart.

Such tragedies might occur less often if we had more smiles and laughter in our lives. A clear, refreshing laugh can flood the home with sunlight. And I would like to see more of us possess the time and willingness to participate wholeheartedly in the joy of others. When one lives in such a way, each day will leave behind it something refreshing and fine. The attitude towards life that seeks always to see the seamier side of people can lead one only to a world of darkness and gloom and will contribute in the end to one's own defeat.

Man is a creature of emotions. His heart and mind are forever in motion. And in these nuances of mood and feeling the human being exists. One therefore cannot afford to be careless in his relations with others. When one is sincere in his consideration for others, in even the most trifling matters, then he can bring about a complete change in the world around him.

For example, when a husband returns home tired from work, the greatest joy for him is to encounter an atmosphere where he can feel really relaxed in heart and mind. If a wife is truly wise, she will take care to see that he is provided with such an atmosphere. In the case of children, the important thing is that parents should at all times appear to them to be fair-minded and without affectations or pretensions. For this reason, it is best that parents think of their children as independent individuals in society, worthy of respect as such and not just because they are one's own children.

To realize the aims I have mentioned above, it is necessary to make every effort possible to perceive and bring out the best qualities in others. People have a tendency, once they have made up their minds on some matter, to become fettered by their own point of view and to find it all but impossible to break free from their prejudices. Such hard-and-fast opinions can often be the cause of quite unexpected ruptures in domestic relations. In order to overcome these prejudices, one must constantly strive to develop the habit not of looking at others from one's own point of view but of looking at oneself from the point of view of others. What is needed is a certain objectivity and breadth in one's outlook. In the end, the important thing is to strive constantly to combat one's inner obstinacy, jealousy, and hatred. And at the same time one must learn to keep in mind that all persons, no matter who they are, have both good points and bad.

In closing, I would like to quote a section from a letter my teacher Jōsei Toda wrote to a relative in 1938. He said: "Human life is not a sad affair. It is possible to enjoy life regardless of where you live, what kind of house you live in, what food you eat or what clothes you wear. If you understand the law of life, then life can be happy. Do not become emotional about anything. Do not be afraid of anything. In all things, use your intellect and power of reason. Let your life be imbued with feelings that are based upon pure love."

The letter was written in the prewar period, when President Toda was thirty-seven. President Toda, along with his teacher Tsunesaburō Makiguchi, had already become a believer in True Buddhism, and it is on that basis that he declares with conviction, "Human life is not a sad affair." This unswerving faith remained with him through the war years, the period of persecution by the militaristic government when he was confined for two years in prison. He could face these difficulties without faltering because the "law of life" was firmly implanted within the depths of his heart. The "law of life," needless to say, is the Buddhist faith. But leaving aside for the moment the matter of religious belief, I would like to point out that his words contain an important statement concerning human life.

"It is possible to enjoy life regardless of where you live, what kind of house you live in, what food you eat or what clothes you wear." People today have a strong tendency to associate happiness with material things —food, clothing, housing—and to seek momentary satisfaction of the senses. To President Toda, such material considerations were no more than external accidents of circumstance. The only true measure of happiness was the sense of living life to the full—such was the conviction that came to him out of the depths of his religious faith.

This, it seems to me, comes close to defining the ultimate meaning of life. And I believe that the "pure love" that characterized the life of President Toda, that allowed him to remain unshaken before every kind of external pressure and trial, and prompted him to love all men, to love life, and to look up to heaven and proclaim the principles of his faith regardless of what hardships he faced—I believe that wonderful "pure love" of his can serve as a vital guide to those who are attempting to make their way through an age of confusion and darkness. Japanese society will no doubt see further waves of trouble and confusion in the years to come. I pray in my heart that all those housewives who must face these difficulties will be able to summon up their courage and wisdom and will succeed in the task of creating happy households and lives based upon firm and unshakable foundations.

MOTHERS

My mother died in September of last year. Her face at the end was smiling and peaceful. She was eighty when she died, so one can say that she lived out her full allotment of years.

I returned to my old home for the wake and the funeral, the first time I had been there for some time. From a conventional point of view, one would hardly say that I was a very dutiful son. I am always so busy with other things that I have little time for personal affairs. It is over sixteen years since I became president of the Sōka Gakkai, and the number of visits I paid to my mother during that time could probably be counted on the fingers of one hand.

My mother seemed to understand the position I am in. Last summer, when her health began to fail, I went to see how she was. As I stood by her bed, she nodded and said, "I'm all right. Don't worry about me. There are lots of people counting on you. You go along to where they are." The summer passed, and as the fall began to deepen, she died, but I can still hear those words of hers echoing in my ear.

My mother was a very ordinary person who seemed content to live a quiet life in her own small corner of the world. And yet from the plain, unassuming way she lived, I know I learned many important things about life.

My mother bore and brought up a number of children. Her old age was peaceful enough, but in her younger days I know she faced many hardships. She overcame them silently and patiently through sheer effort and hard work. And I remember that she always used to say, "Children are a gift from Heaven."

155

She wasn't the only one to say that, of course. People of her generation always used to speak of children as a "gift from Heaven." It's an expression that conveys a sense of respect and tenderness toward life. And it also implies a deep respect for the universe that creates and sustains human life.

According to recent reports, in America these days the babies of unwed mothers, instead of being put up for adoption through legally recognized agencies, are sometimes sold on a kind of adoption "black market." Have the times changed so much, or have human beings themselves changed? Whatever the explanation, it is shocking news. According to one survey, more than five thousand babies were sold in the adoption black market in the course of one year. That such a thing should occur in a materially and culturally advanced nation like the United States makes it particularly ominous.

For some time now, there has been talk of child abuse and the growing dearth of genuine motherly love, and unfortunately Japan seems to be a leader in the trend. I recall reading four or five years ago that Tokyo was far ahead of New York in the number of mothers who did away with their own newborn babies.

Whereas in the past, children were a gift given to one, now they are something to be "made" or "not made" as one chooses. And, the arrogance of human nature being what it is, this awareness of freedom of choice in the creation of children in time leads, it would seem, to a feeling that children are one's own personal possession and therefore may be treated any way one likes.

In the past, maternal affection was thought to be a natural part of a woman's makeup. But the recent unusual happenings I have referred to already call that into question. And we cannot dismiss the problem simply by saying that these occurrences represent a failure of the normal maternal instinct. Frankly speaking, what they represent is a kind of deadening of the awareness of life itself.

The earth and the universe which we inhabit constitute one great living entity made up of the harmony and interplay of various life forces, and these have been in existence from long ages past. Human life reposes in this great sea of life that is the universe. The men and women of today, it appears to me, must learn to see human life in these terms and to recover a sense of reverence for it.

Buddhism, with its view of the eternal continuity of life, teaches that human beings keep passing through various states of existence, and that all the men and women alive in the world today were at some time in the past our own parents. Therefore, if we treat even one of these human beings with disrespect, we can never attain Buddhahood—that is, we can never become a complete human being. Buddhism, in its quest for the reality of human life, teaches us to adopt an attitude of humility, treating others with loving kindness and learning to understand how their lives are intertwined with our own. And I am confident that the wisdom of Buddhism, which has for so many centuries been an underlying part of the history of Asia, holds an enormous significance for the men and women of our time, suffering as they do from spiritual desolation. For through it they will come to realize that, when they fail to respect the individual nature of their children or to treat them with tenderness, they are in fact doing violence to the sanctity of their own lives.

People often say, "The parent who raised you means more to you than the parent who bore you." There is a great deal of meaning in these words. Just bearing a child does not make one a mother. Motherhood, or parenthood, I would like to think, means raising a child with genuine affection and, on the part of both parent and child, cherishing the precious gift of life that has been given them.

The poet Hakushū Kitahara has written that "a mother's milk is softer than the flesh of the loquat, sweeter than the citron." When he was a child, Kitahara is said to have been so delicate that he would run a fever on the slightest exposure to the open air. As a young man, he defied his father's wishes and left home to go to Tokyo. At that time, his mother prepared clothing and bedding for him and secretly helped him to run away from home. The fact that in his later years he became a distinguished poet is said to have been due to her influence.

I too had very delicate health when I was a child, and once, when I was in my teens, I was on the point of entering a sanatorium for tubercular patients. The thing about me that my mother worried most over was my health. After I became a disciple of President Jōsei Toda and he was encountering great difficulty, I left home and went to live in a lodging house. I had only one small room, facing north, but my mother would unobtrusively help me out by sending someone to do my laundry and fix meals for me. For that reason, I can understand how Kitahara felt about his mother.

For a time I edited a young people's magazine in President Toda's publishing house. Also, under the pen name Shin'ichirō Yamamoto, I had occasion to write a biography of the famous Swiss educator J. H. Pestalozzi. Pestalozzi said that the home is like a school and the mother is the most important teacher in it. He also said that the child learns from the actions of the mother. Before anyone is aware of it, the figure of the mother becomes reflected in the figure of the child. That is why I hope the mothers of today will do all they can at home to instill in their children a habit of thoroughgoing respect for others. But if a mother is constantly saying bad things about others, how can she expect to raise a child who is generous and broad-minded? How can a mother who is always looking down on other people's shortcomings hope to raise a child who respects the good points of others? The daily actions and attitudes of the mother foreshadow the future of the child. Therefore a mother who is cheerful and forward-looking in her attitude toward life, even though she may be a quite ordinary person, imparts to her child a spiritual treasure worth more than anything else she could give.

Education begins on the mother's knee, and all the words that a child hears in its early years go to form its character—such was the opinion of the famous British scientist Sir John Barrow. It seems to me a very apt observation. After one has grown up, how often one finds oneself unexpectedly recalling the happy days of childhood spent with one's mother. The general framework of one's personality, habits, and wisdom are formed in the early years through contact with the mother, and remain with one later in the form of a store of memories.

I too have a number of my mother's words stored up in the back of my mind, and at times they light up with a sparkle like diamonds. Even now, I believe, the things my mother said and did continue to exercise an unconscious influence over me. The image of her that dwells in my mind helps to ease the fatigue of my work and to give me the determination I need to face the coming day.

The things I remember her saying, when it comes down to it, were quite commonplace. "Never be a burden to others." "Never tell a lie." I'm sure all mothers must say the same thing. And I recall too, when I was entering boyhood, how she said, "If you make up your mind to do something, then see it through to the end in a responsible manner." She doesn't seem to have been the kind of mother who had great dreams for my future or thought a lot about what schools I should attend. She was an ordinary mother who said very ordinary things. And yet her words stick in my mind because, as in the case of most people, I suppose, I remember the warmth and affection with which she said them.

Speaking of the influences, seen and unseen, that mothers exert on their children, I am reminded of the pleasant conversations I had with the late Count R. E. Coudenhove-Kalergi, the leading proponent of European unity. We met several times when he was in Japan. As most people are aware, I believe, his mother was a Japanese woman of the Meiji period.

In the course of our discussions I asked him about his impressions of Japanese women. As though calling up memories from the distant past, he answered in a tone of deep seriousness. "The only Japanese woman I ever really knew was my mother," he said. "My father died when she was quite young. She had seven children, including myself, and she raised them all by herself. Throughout her life she loved Japanese music, and she was also talented in painting. She was a woman of great artistic sensibility. In educating her children, she did her best to carry on in the same spirit as my father. We were brought up not as Japanese but as Europeans."

Then he added with conviction, "If it had not been for my mother, I'm sure I would never have initiated the movement for European unity." As a matter of fact, she has been acclaimed as one of the founding spirits behind the European Economic Community. I doubt that there are many Japanese women who have been so highly honored.

She was widowed after fourteen years of married life, and in spite of numerous difficulties, succeeded in raising her seven children in admirable fashion. Though she herself was an old-fashioned Meiji type woman, she made a determined effort to acquaint herself with European culture and to become a European herself so that she could bring up her children as full-fledged Europeans. She appears to have been a woman of indomitable spirit, who took pride in her Japanese ancestry and was determined never to do anything that would disgrace it. It is not difficult to imagine

159

how a mother of such character could create a rich spiritual climate for her children. With such a background, we can understand how her son in time could conceive the ideal of a Pan-Europeanism transcending national and cultural boundaries.

She believed that any woman who could be laughed at by her own children because of her ignorance was not qualified to be a mother. For that reason, she studied along with her children, taking care to keep a month ahead of them in their lessons so that she could give them proper guidance. Her children, we are told, respected her deeply for the unusual efforts this cost her. And in the course of assisting her children in their education, she at the same time made herself a more mature and broad-minded woman. Because she was this kind of mother, she could shape and give unlimited breadth to the spiritual vision of her son, Count Coudenhove-Kalergi.

All too often today we hear of mothers who abandon their newborn babies in a coin locker, or who for little or no reason punish their children so severely that they bring about the death of the child. I cannot help thinking that the time has come for mothers to reconsider the true meaning of motherhood and to recognize the great power it possesses.

It was with that thought in mind that several years ago I wrote a poem entitled "Mothers." A friend of mine set it to music, and it has been sung on various occasions at functions sponsored by the Women's Division. Though I am sure it is the melody rather than the words that accounts for its popularity, I am told that the women respond in particular to the lines, "If you did not exist in this world, there would be no great earth to return to, and your children would be wanderers forever." I am sure I am not alone in hoping that the mothers of our time will conduct themselves with pride and confidence, as expressed in the song.

Basically, it makes little sense to talk of good mothers or bad mothers. All mothers have loving arms and brave hearts, have they not? What counts is how broad the mother's outlook is. If we only had more mothers who could see other people's children through the same loving eyes that they see their own children, how peaceful the world would become! In this connection, the legend associated with Kishimojin, the Indian goddess of childbirth, has much to teach us.

Kishimojin was originally cruel and barbarous in nature. She is said to have had five hundred children, but to have made a practice of seizing and eating the children of others. Shakyamuni Buddha, appalled by such conduct, conceived a plan to lead her to enlightenment. He stole her youngest child Binkara and concealed him from her. Kishimojin, half mad with worry, searched everywhere for the child, and finally inquired if the Buddha knew anything about him.

"Kishimojin," he said, "you have five hundred children, yet when you lose even one of them, you wail and lament, do you not? If that is the kind of motherly love you possess, then how can you go on snatching other people's children away from them one after another? If a mother who has only two or three children is deprived of one of them, her grief must be even greater than yours!" At these words of the Buddha, we are told, Kishimojin repented and reformed her ways.

Thus it is that Buddhism teaches us the proper way to live. If the mother who thinks only of her own child can learn to extend that same love to other human beings as well, she will find herself liberated from her former blind love and attachment. These days, we occasionally encounter mothers who look after their children with the kind of blind affection that marked Kishimojin before her enlightenment, but such narrow-minded love is in no sense a blessing to the child. If there is one kind of mother that I do not like, it is the kind who is always boasting about her own children. The legend of Kishimojin is designed to show us the folly of such narrow-mindedness.

A mother's love, they say, is deeper than the sea, but I hope sincerely that it will not remain the kind of blind affection I have spoken of. Only when such affection becomes the basis for a broader compassion, extended to all persons without distinction, can it be called true maternal love. When a mother has that kind of broad compassion and tenderness, then she will be able to guide her children as a parent should and bring them up to be fine individuals, and in the process, she herself will grow in stature and maturity. She will have found the true path of life.

A well-known founder of a women's college has stated that the aims of women's education should be to train women first as human beings, second as women, and third as mothers. Here I would like to stress the fact that the primary objective is the education of women as human beings. Before one considers how to train women or mothers, one must consider how to turn out fine individuals, for that is the lifetime goal of education.

Of course, one's life as a woman and a mother is not completely divorced from one's life as an individual. The manner in which one lives as an individual and a human being is, on the contrary, the foundation that underlies the other phases and modes of life. If that foundation is firmly established, a woman will be able to watch her children grow up and leave home, or to face personal tragedy such as the death of her husband, without undue despair, because she knows how to go on living as a person.

The woman who strives in her own way to do the best she can for her husband, for her children, and for those around her, deserves the highest praise. To live such a life, ordinary though it may be, is a noble thing. And for a mother, there is no greater happiness than to contribute to the welfare of society by devoting her life to raising her children and preparing them for a role in the world.

My mother is no longer alive, but that was how she spent her life, laboring over the years to bring up healthy children and send them out into the world. And in my heart, I know that my mother's life, commonplace though it was, was one of victory.

ADVICE TO NEWLYWEDS

We're into a new year. I know there must be many newly married couples who are celebrating their first New Year's together. We hear a great deal about the so-called new style families these days, though it's hard to tell how much of it one should believe. However, over half the population in Japan today was born in the postwar era, and young people keep getting married and setting up new households. It is these young people who are eagerly working to establish their own families that I would like to call "new families" here.

How did these new families spend the New Year's? Perhaps they didn't indulge in all the traditional New Year's pastimes, such as sitting around the footwarmer and eating New Year's delicacies, or playing shuttlecock or parcheesi, though I doubt that they forgot about them entirely. Perhaps, to get away from their cramped living quarters, they took the children and went downtown or visited their parents' home. There were some, perhaps, who decided to splurge and go off to a quiet hot spring in the mountains to see the new year in. And I expect there were plenty who complained that, with times as hard as they are now, it is impossible to get into a proper New Year's mood anyway.

A well-known writer, describing the excitement and bewilderment of newly married life, said that it is like "watching with fascination as a little boat glides smoothly over a lake in the direction of happiness, and then getting into a boat of your own and trying to do the same." This strikes me as a very ingenious comparison. All young people, before they are married, dream of building a happy home. Such dreams are in a sense like gazing at a little boat gliding over a lake. But when they themselves get into a boat and start out, they discover it takes considerable practice just to be able to manage the oars. And the surface of the lake, it turns out, is not always as smooth as a mirror. Sometimes there are high winds and rains and sudden squalls. In the case of an actual boat trip, one can always turn around and head back to shore when dangers threaten. But in the figurative journey we are talking about, the journey of married life, there is no turning back. And when the trouble leads to divorce, then all parties are the losers.

The reader may object that this is a very inauspicious subject to be talking about so soon after the beginning of the new year. But statistics show that the divorce rate in Japan is increasing. Moreover, roughly half of the divorces take place within the first five years of marriage, a point I find particularly disturbing. I'm sure all the parties involved have their reasons. I am not trying to offer any blanket condemnation of their actions. What I cannot help but feel apprehensive over is the fact that so many of the divorces these days are attributed to incompatibility due to personality differences. Just how hard, I wonder, do the two young people try in their efforts to make a success of their marriage.

Last fall I read in a magazine about how many people have been going to the Pokkuri Temple recently to pray. In case you are not familiar with it, the Pokkuri Temple is a temple in Nara Prefecture where people go to pray that they will not become a burden to others in their old age but will die *pokkuri*—that is, "pop off" suddenly and painlessly. The article explained that the type of people who come to the temple has changed markedly in the last few years. In the past it was mainly very old people who came to pray. But recently there have been more people of a somewhat younger age, in particular women in their forties or fifties. The overall number of visitors to the temple has also increased. Whereas in the past the temple may have had no more than four or five busloads of worshipers in the course of a year, now as many as ten busloads may appear in a single day.

With these changes has come a change in the attitude of the people who visit the temple. In the past, if you asked the very old people why they came to pray for a quick and effortless death, they would reply quite frankly: they did not want to be a further burden to the spouse who had already taken such good care of them. Nowadays, one finds an increasing number of middle-aged women who declare flatly, "I don't want to be beholden to anyone!"

I felt rather downcast when I read this part of the article. A woman in her forties or fifties is in a sense in the best years of her life. While in her teens and twenties she has the undeniable charm of youth, it is really only in later years that the depth and beauty of her personality become fully developed. And to find women in that period of life declaring grimly that they "don't want to be beholden to anyone!" strikes one with a painful sense of gloom and loneliness.

My wife and I both are going through the same stage of life as these women, so I can in some degree understand their feelings. People in Japan who are now in their forties or fifties in their young days all had to face the grim fact of their country's defeat in the Pacific War. And in the postwar period they experienced a sudden overturning of all the traditional values of Japanese life. It was a time of want and hardship, when one had to struggle just to stay alive. The people of that age group were the ones who created the affluent and highly developed society of present-day Japan. And women played a vital role in that process, though their contribution may be less apparent than that of the male population. After all the hardships the men and women of that generation went through, one wonders why they should have to face this gloom and loneliness in their later years. They are the fathers and mothers of the newlyweds I talked of previously. I cannot help feeling that the generation gap between parents and children has brought about a degree of alienation that is deeper than anyone would have expected.

The very old people declare that they do not want to be a further burden to the spouses who have already taken such good care of them. The members of the next generation assert that they do not want to be beholden to anyone at all. What an enormous difference there is in the two pronouncements. The first, for all its tragic undertones, conveys a sense of human warmth and tenderness. The second suggests a mood of desolation, deeper than what we ordinarily speak of as alienation, and seems almost to welcome the prospect of death. Why should such an air of darkness have descended upon the members of that generation? It is a question I would like the newlywed couples to think about carefully.

Of course, I do not suppose that these symptoms have afflicted all the members of that generation in every walk of life. And I do not want to appear to be trying to push the whole responsibility for the situation off upon the younger generation. One reason for the change in attitude is no doubt the fact that advances in medical science have lengthened the average span of human life. And even more important is the general mood of bewilderment and stagnation that has invaded present-day society as a whole. At the same time, it is a fact that this very society was created largely by the members of the generation we are speaking about.

I believe, however, that we must look to the future in all things. As the proverb says, the night is darkest just before the dawn. No matter how dark the clouds overshadowing society, somewhere in the sky above them the sun must be shining. The question is whether or not we have faith in its shining and are prepared to take up the challenge and work patiently and strenuously to sweep the clouds away. The leaders in such an effort must be the young people of today, and in particular, the young couples who are now advancing to a position of key importance in society. These young people have about them a sunniness and freedom from care that marks them as quite different from people of my own generation and leads me to put great confidence in them. At the same time, of course, I expect a great deal from them.

When I speak of taking up the challenge, however, I am not advocating the kind of self-sacrificing devotion to the cause that was demanded of the Japanese people during the Pacific War, or the kind of fanatic devotion to company interests that has marked so many young businessmen in the postwar period. Speaking in terms of the family, I would ask only that the young people maintain at all times what I would call an "open family." No human being can live in total isolation. Spatially, we are constantly interacting with society and the world of nature around us. To cite merely one example, it is well known that the circulation of blood in the human body is intimately linked with the movement of the tides. And in temporal terms, the conduct of our lives is deeply influenced by the forces of history and tradition. If we were to try to cut ourselves off from these temporal and spatial forces, our lives would become as lacking in savor as a mouthful of sand. It is when we learn to interact with these two great forces and to maintain a delicate balance between them that we live most fully.

When I look at the young couples of today, I always worry if they are perhaps not in danger of cutting themselves off from the flow of these forces. To put it another way, although there is a fine warmth and frankness among young couples today, as though they were close friends rather than husband and wife, one wonders if they are not running the risk of shutting themselves off from society and living in a private world of their own. Though I may seem to be giving advice where it is not wanted, I wonder if some of the middle-aged women who visit the Pokkuri Temple do not do so out of a sense of rejection and isolation because they have been shut out of the world of their married children.

I have at hand as I write this a letter from a young housewife in Hokkaido. Last year I visited the village of Atsuta in Hokkaido, where my teacher Jōsei Toda lived in his youth, returning with many pleasant memories of the occasion. At that time I happened to meet this young woman and we chatted for a while. Her letter mentions her impressions of the meeting and conveys news of more recent happenings.

Among other things, she reports that she has been very busy with preparations for the long Hokkaido winter. These include drying potatoes, onions, and carrots in the sun and storing them away in the cellar, and making various kinds of pickles. In the region where she lives, the older women play a very active role in teaching the younger wives how to make pickles and take other steps to get through the winter in comfort. The younger ones for their part do what they can to keep the older women informed on recent developments and other matters that they might not know about. As I read the letter, I couldn't help smiling at the picture of the older wives, their sleeves tucked up, bustling around and vigorously directing activities.

I think there is a very important lesson to be learned from this report. It is that among the traditions and customs of the common people, deeply rooted as they are in the earth itself, there are many types of knowledge and skill that cannot be gained from books. Such knowledge can be learned only through direct contact with others. It is like a bodily warmth which passes from one person to another. Such wisdom can remain alive only so long as there is close contact between members of different generations.

Not only this type of wisdom, but all knowledge, one might say, must be transmitted in this way. We have for a long time heard complaints about the shortcomings of our modern mass production techniques of education. Their principal failing seems to be a lack of human warmth. By that I mean the kind of warmth that existed in the little, privately run village schools of Japan in earlier centuries, in which not only the knowledge but the experience and character of the teacher were transmitted to his pupils. It was what you might call a handmade education. And because the knowledge taught was imbued with this human warmth, it could be absorbed by the pupils and transformed into the type of wisdom that could play a vital role in their lives. The young housewife of Hokkaido, of course, did not go so far as to say all this in her letter. But I am quite sure that in the pickling instructions she received from some wrinkled old lady, she acquired almost by instinct an invaluable lesson in the wisdom of daily life.

As times change, it is natural that certain things about the life of the housewife will change too. But I believe there are also things about a wife's role that must never change. Among these the most important are the invisible family ties that bind husband and wife, parent and child together as human beings. These ties are not something that exist apart from society as a whole. They are part of a web of ties, spatially linking together the individual, the family, and society, and temporally tying up with the history and traditions of the past.

As I have said, a young husband and wife are so engrossed in their own personal relationship that they tend to break away from the ties of tradition and other personal relationships and to create a private world of their own. For a time this may strike them as an exemplary solution and they may feel great relief at having escaped from the bother of complicated relationships with others. But they will find that this sense of tranquility is short-lived. A young couple may feel that by isolating themselves, they can escape from the interference of their parents. Before long their own children begin to grow up and they learn what it means to be in the parents' position. When young married people make no effort to strengthen and broaden their ties with others, they will find some minor disagreement weighing more and more heavily upon them until it leads to a major and irreversible family breakup, such as a rupture between husband and wife or between parents and children. The increase in the divorce rate and the sudden popularity of visits to the Pokkuri Temple—these two phenomena, I believe, are by no means unrelated to one another. Certain ties in society underlie the foundations of life itself. These ties have now begun to break apart. This has come about because of the disintegration of the family system, which I believe is one of the most serious problems facing Japanese society today.

You may think I mean that newlyweds ought to live with their parents. I am, however, proposing no such simplistic solution. Families differ greatly in their makeup and habits, as well as in the amount of living space available to them, and no blanket rule can be laid down on how they should live. The point I am trying to stress here is that as long as people live in society, they must learn to expect and cope with a certain amount of trouble and discord. Society is a place in which the older generation and the younger generation, old ways of living and new ways, tradition and innovation, rights and duties, self-assertion and self-denial, all exist side by side, interacting with one another and in time achieving some degree of balance and order. But because it is such a place, it is inevitably marked by a certain amount of friction and discord. No one can escape from such troubles, no matter how he may try.

If there are any newlyweds who naively believe they can sail through life and somehow avoid all trouble, I am afraid that the little boat they are riding in will overturn the moment it encounters so much as a light gale. They will find their youth fading away all too soon, their hopes dimming, until in time, amid grumbling and discontent, they are forced to admit the utter failure of their lives. This is something I would not under any circumstances want to see happen to the young people of today.

For that reason, I would like to stress here that true happiness is not to be found in luxury and outward show. For such outward show, however it may shine and sparkle, is empty of love and human warmth.

I am reminded of the Pushkin masterpiece *Eugene Onegin*, which I read when I was young. As you know, the narrative deals with the Russian ruling class and exposes the ennui and intellectual emptiness hidden beneath the surface glitter of aristocratic society. The hero, Onegin, is a typical product of that society. In an effort to relieve his boredom, he throws himself into the pursuit of pleasure. He meets and becomes attracted to Tatiana, a simplehearted daughter of the country gentry, and soon they fall passionately in love. But for Onegin, the young girl's innocent devotion is no more than a passing diversion. Though he speaks in the manner of an older brother, admonishing her that he is unworthy of her love, his words betray a coldhearted attitude. Tatiana's love goes unrequited and Onegin departs from the scene. In her despair, Tatiana consents to marry a man she does not love.

Some years later, Onegin, still unmarried, happens to meet Tatiana again. She is now the wife of Count N. and a figure of prominence in polite society. When Onegin begs her to love him as she once did, she replies tearfully with words to this effect: "Of what value to me is this luxury and the odious ostentation of high class society, of success in social circles, of fashionable mansions and lavish parties? I would gladly exchange these masquerade-ball clothes, this brilliance and bustle and breathtaking pace for the shelf of books, the overgrown garden, the poor house, the place where I lived when I first met you. Happiness was before our very eyes then. It was so close we could have reached out and grasped it."

To me, these last words are unforgettable, for they state the case precisely. True happiness does not exist in some far-off realm, but right in the place where you are. It does not do to pursue some kind of phantom life, seeking to avoid all troubles and forever chasing after dreams. If one will learn to face the reality of each new day and to overcome all difficulties, then one is bound to discover the true nature of happiness. That is why I would like to see young newlyweds learn the joy of helping one another and working to build a solid foundation for their lives.

I am sometimes invited to attend the weddings and receptions, the starting line of married life for these new couples. Most of the time I am so busy with other affairs that I have to beg off with a telegram of congratulations. Sometimes, however, I write a few words on a plaque and send it as a present. Visualizing the future that lies ahead of the young couple, I often write the words, "Two people—a cherry tree." Just as the cherry tree grows from a little sapling into a beautiful blooming tree, so I hope that the newlyweds will establish a family that will be a true ornament to society, not shutting themselves off from the world but joining their strength to conquer all difficulties and live lives of victory.

170

As time goes on, the prime concern of these new couples will probably become the question of how to educate their children. It is often asserted that young mothers today have lost confidence in their ability to bring up and educate their children. I do not necessarily think this is so, though it is true that we see, on the one hand, examples of mothers who are overly protective of their children, and on the other hand, those who appear to have lost all trace of maternal instinct. Nowadays, when we hear so often of mothers who abandon or even kill their newborn infants, I feel it is imperative that we consider once again the true meaning of the word mother.

I would like to call upon the young mothers of Japan to regain the courage and confidence necessary to raise their children through their own innate wisdom. That wisdom may be very simple, it may be one-sided, but if it is a wisdom that the mother has acquired through her own experiences in life, if it is a product of her own vitality and being, then I know it will suffice.

Here I would like to relate the experiences of a friend of mine named Mrs. N. She was trained as a nurse and in time married a doctor. Tragedy struck shortly after. Mrs. N. lost her eyesight as a result of cerebral hemorrhages. Divorce followed, and she was left with an infant son to raise. She faced a truly forbidding future, and turned in her need to religion. After three years, she regained her eyesight to some degree and began a period of long and intense struggle to make her way in life. She managed to find work as a nurse, but as there was no one she could leave her child with, she often had to take him along, fixing a place for him to sleep in the X-ray room where she worked. For ten years and more, she lived a life of poverty and hardship. She could not buy her little boy the toys she would like to have given him, or provide him with a room of his own to study in, but somehow, through the sheer power of love, she managed to bring him up.

Later, when I heard that her son had passed the government legal examination and embarked on a career in law, I felt as though I were listening to Mrs. N.'s song of victory. I was even more moved when I saw the poem entitled "For Mother" which the young man wrote when he was a child. Since it was not intended for publication in the first place, we need not concern ourselves here with the question of its literary merit.

What is important is the deep feeling in the poem; it cannot help but strike the heart of the reader. With the family's permission, I would like to quote from it.

> *Mother, how gentle you are.*
> *Mother, how strict you are.*
> *When I'm stuck, you encourage me and tell me not to give up.*
> *When I manage to do something right, you cry because you're*
> *so happy.*
>
> *Sometimes we had fights*
> *and I thought, I never want to see her again!*
> *But she's my mother, the only one I have.*
> *But Mother, there are things I have to do.*
> *The time will come when I must strike out on my own.*
> *When that time comes, please see me off with a smile.*
> *And please believe that, wherever I go, I'll be thinking of you.*
> *Someday the two of us will walk side by side again.*
> *So, please live a long time,*
> *please live to be a hundred!*
> *That's my wish, and meanwhile I'll do my best.*
> *I'll do my best—just watch me, Mother!*

Perhaps this mother wasn't able to buy any presents for her son. But the son learned many things from her. He learned, did he not, how fine a thing it is to do one's very best in life?

Mrs. N., as it happens, belongs to an older generation than that of the newlyweds I have been talking about. But there is something in her story that transcends generation barriers. I hope the young people of today, as they face life's ups and downs and grow older year by year, will live in such a way that they can look back later and say with satisfaction, "We did our best!"